teach yourself®

**running your own
business**

**running your own
business**
kevin duncan

The publisher has used its best endeavours to ensure that the URLs for external websites referred to in this book are correct and active at the time of going to press. However, the publisher and the author have no responsibility for the websites and can make no guarantee that a site will remain live or that the content will remain relevant, decent or appropriate.

For UK order enquiries: please contact Bookpoint Ltd, 130 Milton Park, Abingdon, Oxon, OX14 4SB. Telephone: +44 (0) 1235 827720. Fax: +44 (0) 1235 400454. Lines are open 09.00–17.00, Monday to Saturday, with a 24-hour message answering service. Details about our titles and how to order are available at www.teachyourself.co.uk

Long renowned as the authoritative source for self-guided learning – with more than 50 million copies sold worldwide – the **teach yourself** series includes over 500 titles in the fields of languages, crafts, hobbies, business, computing and education.

British Library Cataloguing in Publication Data: a catalogue record for this title is available from the British Library.

ISBN-10: 0 340 88689 7
ISBN-13: 978 0340 886892

First published in UK 2005 by Hodder Arnold, 338 Euston Road, London, NW1 3BH.

This edition published 2005.

The **teach yourself** name is a registered trade mark of Hodder Headline Ltd.

Copyright © 2005 Kevin Duncan

Typeset by Transet Limited, Coventry, England.
Printed in Great Britain for Hodder Education, a division of Hodder Headline, 338 Euston Road, London NW1 3BH, by Cox & Wyman Ltd, Reading, Berkshire.

Hodder Headline's policy is to use papers that are natural, renewable and recyclable products and made from wood grown in sustainable forests. The logging and manufacturing processes are expected to conform to the environmental regulations of the country of origin.

Impression number   10 9 8 7 6 5
Year   2010 2009 2008 2007

contents

dedication

This book is dedicated to my father James Grant Duncan, 1923–1989. Although he hasn't been around for a while, much of the advice in this book is based on his philosophy of life.

The book is also dedicated to my daughters Rosanna and Shaunagh. Maybe one day you'll need it girls.

acknowledgements

This book began life when someone suggested that I should write my advice down instead of just telling people what to do. Some notes became a pamphlet, which in turn became a book. Thanks to everyone who commented on it or read a draft, in particular Sarah Taylor, and Rassami and Niclas Hök Ljungberg. And thanks to Robert Ashton for the initial contact.

about the author

Kevin Duncan worked in advertising and direct marketing for 20 years. For the last five years he has worked on his own as a marketing consultant. He is an adviser to various businesses in design, public relations, advertising and accountancy, helping them with business strategy, marketing and training.

He has two daughters, Rosanna and Shaunagh, and lives in Westminster. In his spare time he travels to strange parts of the world, collects classic guitars and flies birds of prey.

He can be contacted at:
kevinduncan@expertadvice.co.uk

or you can look at his website:
www.expertadviceonline.com

introduction

Lots of books tell you how to deal with the practicalities. This one tells you how to deal with yourself.

It is a fairly simple matter to walk into a bookshop and pick up a whole range of books on the practical aspects of setting up your own business. You know the sort of thing – clever ways to arrange your financial systems, how to organize your filing, tips on how to win customers, and so on.

Yet it is significantly harder to find something that helps you to deal with your own frame of mind. When you do actually start running your own business, the first thing that you have to confront is that the whole thing is down to *you*. This is not a one-off sensation that only occurs at the beginning. In fact, it never quite goes away, even after you have had a successful start and have established a bank of regular customers.

Over the last five years I have often found myself discussing this feeling with friends and colleagues who work on their own. Discussions became tangible ideas, and some were written down. A checklist became a pamphlet, which became a small book. It then doubled in size.

What has emerged is 110 ways to help increase your chances of independent success. All the suggestions here have been test-driven by the author or a respected colleague. They are written in a pragmatic and sympathetic style by someone who has done it himself.

We owe it to ourselves to make business enjoyable even if the central reason for it is to make money. The central principle of this book is that working on your own doesn't mean that you are destined to feel lonely or isolated. It can actually be the best feeling in the world. Free of the constraints of company life, or brimming with enthusiasm at the prospect of at last being able to realize the benefits of your own idea, you are all set to experience the thrill of being your own boss.

Learn how to motivate yourself, adopt successful habits, and stay sane

So now you have total responsibility. That's right, *total responsibility*. The glory is all yours when things go well, and of course the problems are all yours when they don't. Therefore, as well as being a hugely rewarding experience, it can also be a very scary state of affairs – a world where there never seems to be a weekend because you can't stop thinking about a problem or fretting over where the next payment is coming from.

Nevertheless, with a sound business idea and the right approach, millions have already shown that you can definitely run a successful business and have a better balanced personal life as a result. That means a much fairer equation between the effort you put in and the reward you get out, whether that is financial or emotional.

What can never truly be quantified is the degree to which people who run their own business really enjoy this level of autonomy and revel in the freedom it brings, or quietly find it a constant daily struggle. Perhaps the answer will always be a little bit of both.

What is certainly true is that being organized, thinking ahead and learning to switch off are some of the qualities that those who work on their own must master. While many books are filled with technical advice on running the practical side of your own business, few of them delve into the more tricky area of how to deal with your emotions.

This book attends to what are sometimes called the softer issues: how to conduct yourself; how to understand why other people behave as they do; ensuring that their actions don't upset you unduly; establishing how to do the things you don't like without becoming unbearably grumpy; and so on. In short, how to be successful *and* stay sane.

Learn how to take the issues seriously, but not yourself

A huge proportion of the country now works from home in one form or another, whether they use their home as an office, or run their own business from a shop or workshop. They are used to the reaction 'You work for yourself? That's great.' But many end up walking away from such a conversation thinking: 'If only they knew the headaches involved.'

Once you have made the decision to run your own business, where do you start? What happens if you are halfway through something and encounter an issue you had not expected? What do you do if things aren't going quite as you had planned? How do you have a discussion about resolving a business problem with a colleague or partner if you don't have one?

This book is intended to help all those people who have decided to go solo. It is designed to be your business companion. It has been written by someone who actually does work on his own, and so has experienced most of the issues you are likely to face. Someone who knows the joy of a satisfied client, the personal pride in a job well done, or a cheque arriving on the doormat whose value truly reflects your individual contribution.

Teach Yourself Running your own Business helps to prepare you for the unknown and to make running your own business more of a pleasure.

It's a little like having a business partner who has already been through what you are likely to face next. A large number of the mistakes have already been made for you and some of the lessons learnt, hopefully saving you a large amount of the hassle. The book also frequently lends a humorous angle to take the edge off some of the trickier issues you are likely to encounter. Dip into it frequently.

Oh, and one final thing. Running your own business is all about self-confidence. It is essential that you believe that you are good at what you do. Equally, you will never be perfect so don't beat yourself up if you don't do everything that this book suggests, or if you do things very differently.

Do it your way and make it work for you. Because that's what working on your own is all about.

Summary: who is this book aimed at?

You should read this book if:

- You are thinking of running your own business
- You are already running your own business but you are finding it a bit of a struggle
- You are having trouble motivating yourself
- You are frustrated with books that only deal with the practicalities rather than the emotional issues
- You work for a company but wish to harness some of the qualities of someone who works on their own.

Kevin Duncan, Westminster, 2005

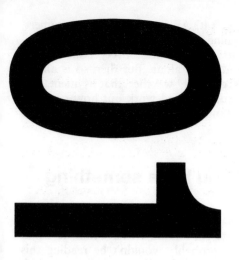

01

where do I start?

In this chapter you will learn
- how to be honest with yourself
- what you need to prepare in order to be a success
- how to write a simple, realistic plan
- how to work out the materials that you need
- how to get it all under way

It's a daunting prospect, isn't it? An empty desk, no customers, no confirmed money coming in, and no one to gossip with. Welcome to running your own business. Every issue is now yours to wrestle with, and yours alone. But then so is all the satisfaction when things go well, whether that is mental or financial. So let's dive straight in and work out how on earth you are going to turn what many would regard as an ordeal into a fantastic success.

1 Assume that you have something to offer

Let's start by assuming that there is a market for your talents, otherwise you wouldn't have got this far. We have to believe that this is true otherwise you probably wouldn't be reading this book. By now you will have established the basics in your mind. Your thought pattern will have been something along the lines of:

- I am good at what I do
- There is a market for my product/service (whether this is actually true and how you set about proving it to yourself will come later (p.8)
- I can do it better on my own than in my current set-up
- I have a way of doing it that people will like
- What I put in and what I get out will be a better balanced equation than my current state of affairs.

That should just about cover it. Thousands of people go through this basic thought process at some point in their working lives – sometimes on many occasions. However, even if you have been able to tick all the boxes so far, the issue that you have to grapple with next is far more fundamental:

> *'If I ran my own business, I'm not sure if I could live with myself.'*

What do people mean when they say this? Well first, there are important issues with regard to exactly where you are going to do your work. What are your domestic arrangements? Could they possibly accommodate you achieving everything that you need to without disrupting all the other aspects of your life?

Second, there is your frame of mind: are you cut out to operate outside of a conventional office environment? Could you cope without the interaction? Could you motivate yourself when no one is there to give you a kick-start?

Evidence suggests that the majority of people are very capable of working on their own. They simply need a little guidance and encouragement to point them in the right direction. If you don't make the leap, you'll never know, so let's make a start.

It is essential that you feel good about yourself. You must genuinely believe that you can offer something of value to others, otherwise you would not have taken the plunge to set up on your own, or even be toying with the idea. Make this vital assumption and start from there. Don't be apologetic about your skills, either to yourself or to a potential customer. State them clearly, get used to saying them out loud, and become comfortable with explaining them to others. Without being arrogant, everyone who works on their own has to have a certain level of self-confidence. You no longer have colleagues to witness your performance and help you with encouraging observations. You rarely get debriefed objectively on how something has gone. Consequently, you have to be very adept at self-assessment. Now all the motivation has to come from within.

2 Be honest with yourself

Do remember, however, that confidence can be misplaced. In fact, over-confidence could beguile you into believing that you have a viable idea or a pleasant way of doing things when you don't. Confront your own hubris and work it out privately before it trips you up.

You work for yourself now, so you don't have to pretend about anything. In truth, you mustn't ever stray into the realms of fantasy because you would only be fooling yourself if you did. From now on it is your job to be sensible and realistic. Do not exaggerate your potential or delude yourself that you can do all sorts of things that you cannot. Equally, do not be sheepish about your skills. You will need to get used to showing a fascinating blend of confidence and humility. It is perfectly fine to have a different external persona, but make sure that you are honest with yourself and that you know your true self.

Consider your position with extreme care and as much objectivity as you can muster. Ask yourself:

- What are you good at?
- How much is that worth to someone else?
- How much will someone pay for what you have to offer?
- Is that enough for you to live on, or to satisfy your ambitions?

Get a piece of paper. Write down what you want to do in your business. Consider it for a while, and then decide whether anyone else would agree with you. This is the beginning of establishing whether there is indeed a market for what you do. Go for a walk. When you come back, look at your piece of paper again. Is it any good? Is it nonsense? If so, write a new one. Stick it on the wall and live with it for a few days. Does it still make sense? Is it rubbish? Does everyone else claim the same thing? What's so different about the way that you would run your business?

These early enquiries are really important. They are the starting point of you being able to have a board meeting with yourself. A degree of schizophrenia here is essential. One half of your mind needs to be capable of putting forward an idea, and the other half needs to be smart enough to confirm or reject it without upsetting yourself in the process. That's no easy matter. So practise debating things on your own, weighing up the pros and cons, reaching a sensible conclusion, deciding what to do next, and remaining calm and objective throughout the whole process.

3 Research your market thoroughly

If you think you have an excellent idea, the first essential thing to do is to research your market thoroughly. Actually it isn't simply one thing to do – it's a lot of things. Try asking yourself these sorts of questions:

- What demand is there for what you provide?
- If you are producing a product, who wants to buy it?
- If you are providing a service, who needs it?
- Who else in the area does this already? (This could be geographical, or sector-based)
- Are they a success? If so, why?
- Are they a failure? If so, what does that tell you?
- What price can you put on your product or service?
- Does that represent a going concern or will you be hard-pushed to make a living?

- What outside factors are you subject to?
- Can you influence these factors or are you totally at their mercy?
- If you have no control over them, does that make the whole venture too vulnerable?
- If you were someone else, would you honestly embark on this venture?
- Why?

The questions are endless, but one of the best pieces of advice here is to be like an inquisitive child and always ask 'Why?' three times in relation to every question. Or, if you are inclined to overstate the potential of everything because you are so enthusiastic about it, ask someone else to ask *you* 'Why?' in relation to all your assertions about how this venture is definitely going to be a roaring success from day one. There is absolutely nothing wrong with oodles of enthusiasm at this stage. Actually, it is an essential prerequisite if you are to be a solo success, but the business won't succeed on enthusiasm alone if it is not tempered with some good old-fashioned realism. If you are a hopeless dreamer, get the reality mongers in to check if you are heading off on a wild goose chase that could end in disaster. This will soon establish whether or not you are deluding yourself.

4 Work out how much money you need

This sounds like a no-brainer, but it is amazing how many people don't really cover the groundwork in this area. What is required here is not a forest of spreadsheets – just a really clear impression of how your business will work financially. Put simply, there are three types of money that you will need:

1 Investment at the start
2 Monthly cash flow
3 The profit (monthly or annual).

It is extraordinary how many businesses mess all this up. Here is the layperson's guide to the three types.

Initial investment

Let's look at the investment needed at the start.

- Do you need to put any money in at all at the beginning? Pause on this one for a moment. If the answer is no, then don't do it.
- If you do need to borrow from some other source, what demands will the lenders make on getting it back? Banks want interest. Investors want cash back. They don't lend money out of kindness. It is so easy to be seduced by the sort of macho talk that goes with establishing a business. You know the sort of stuff: 'We've got some seed corn investment from a consortium of city backers', 'The Venture Capital guys are really interested in the idea'. This may make you feel very important, but these people want their money back, and some. And they will want to be involved in the way you run the business. Therefore, if you can do it without them, then do.
- If you do have to put money in yourself, when are you going to get it back? Don't delude yourself by excluding this amount from your assessment of whether the business is going to be a success.

Many self-employed people say that their business is 'successful' whilst simultaneously failing to remind themselves that 'the business' owes them thousands. This may be acceptable in the early stages, but not if there is no likelihood of you being repaid in the foreseeable future.

Monthly cash flow

This is the amount of income you need each month. Write down what you need. Now write down what you think you can get. Then build in time delays for late payment in the early days. (See Chapter 6, 'Understanding time'). This becomes your first cash-flow projection.

This projection has to be very, very realistic. You must have a reasonable level of confidence that it is achievable otherwise you will have a disaster on your hands almost straightaway. You need to distinguish very carefully between income and profit. If you are ever tempted to start calling this income money 'profit', it has all gone wrong. That means it has gone wrong both on paper and in your head. To repeat, this is not profit – it is income. You can have an infinite amount of the stuff and yet still be making a whopping loss. Make sure that you make proper allowance for all the outgoings that may crop up, as well as an amount to pay yourself a salary to keep the wolf from the door.

Another massive pitfall is if you mentally earmark this money to 'mortgage' other costs. In the same way that shopaholics rationalize a purchase by saying 'I didn't spend £300 on that, so I can use it for something else', you must never double-count your money.

Calculate how much you need to make each month. Once you write it down, it is more likely to happen. (This is a general principle that works for almost everything – if you write it down, it is more likely to happen.) You can have a sensible minimum and maximum, but it is better if you have just one figure. Now you have to work out where it's coming from. Write down a realistic list of the value of your income in the first three months. If this turns out to be nonsense, write a more realistic list next time. As you become better at predicting, you will naturally build in time lags to reflect slow decision making and slow payment (see Chapter 6, 'Understanding time').

The profit (monthly or annual)

The final thing to consider is the profit margin. Ask yourself:

- How much is the profit?
- Does it vary depending on what you have sold?
- Does it vary by month or season?
- Does it fluctuate wildly?
- Why?
- What would make it more consistent?
- What would make it higher?
- What are the tolerance levels?
- What is the average target?
- Is that realistic?
- Is it good enough for you?

You need to keep a regular and close eye on this. You also need to have decided whether you need the profit margin monthly, annually or over any other time period.

- If you need the profit margin monthly, does this mean that your business plan does not include an amount for your own salary?
- If so, is that wise or realistic?
- If you can take the profit annually, how are you keeping tabs on the surplus that is (hopefully) building up?
- Can you equate it back to the running monthly amount?

Be aware that if you manage to convince yourself that you can wait quite a long time to realize a certain margin (a year or more), then you may well have a vulnerable business on your hands. Successful businesses make a good margin with almost everything they do, effectively from day one. Consider this carefully. There is no point in driving yourself into the ground all year only to make a few per cent, unless you are extremely happy with the figure that it generates.

The overall rule is to keep all this incredibly simple. The moment you overcomplicate the finances you will lose the plot and probably start talking nonsense about the business, which, as we are beginning to realize, is one of the worst enemies of anyone working on their own.

5 Write a simple, realistic plan

Quite a few diligent sole traders write endless business plans before they start, and there is nothing fundamentally wrong with that. However, a lot of them get so involved in the spreadsheets and the financial projections that they lose sight of the basics. The best business plans can often be written on the back of an envelope, usually in your local café or bar. Try this simple process:

• Write JFMAMJJASOND along the top of the page to represent the 12 months of the year
• Now cross out at least one or two of them because you will be taking some holiday, and in the first year the whole thing will probably grind to a halt when you are not around
• Now write a figure under each month to determine your income
• Put the likely costs under each
• Subtract one from the other and see what you have left
• If you want to be particularly cautious, try crossing out the first three months' income because businesses always take longer to get off the ground than you think
• Now go and do something else for a while
• Come back to your plan and ask yourself again: 'Is this realistic?'

This exercise will tell you something more fundamental than a meeting with the bank or your accountant. It will be a big surprise if you are happy with it first time. In truth, if you are, you should be a little suspicious. Live with it for a while. Try

J	F	M	A	M	J	J	A	S	O	N	D
		X Launch date									
		X Hols					X Hols				
Income			4	4	4	4	0	4	4	4	0
Costs			2	2	2	2	2	2	2	2	2
Profit			2	2	2	2	–2	2	2	2	–2

First year profit: 10
Pessimistic profit assuming no income in first 3 months: 4

A simple plan

again. Make refinements (not on a spreadsheet, just in pen on another envelope). The great joy with this is that, by keeping it simple, you are now able to explain your business plan to anyone who will listen – and that includes you. Consequently, you are less likely to drift away from your main purpose as the months and years pass by. In some business circles, they call this 'focus'. You should call it 'knowing what I am doing'.

Now, assuming that you have concluded that you do indeed have a going concern, there are some things that you will need to get under way.

6 Invest in a distinctive identity

You need to look good. Your company, shop or service needs a memorable name, a good logo, high quality headed paper, good quality signage, and business cards that invoke a reaction. The name may well be your own if you are known in your field. If not, choose something distinctive. Avoid bland sets of initials that no one can remember (such as BLTWP), or hugely cumbersome stacks of names like Jones, Duncan, Taylor, Hatstand European Consolidated & Partners. They are not memorable and they imply a lack of clarity on your part.

Every detail counts. Don't skimp on quality of paper or thickness of business cards. Thin business cards are as weak as a limp handshake. Don't have them printed at a booth in a railway station! Check the spelling and punctuation really carefully on everything you produce. These days, the world appears to be one large typographical error. Don't be part of it.

What many business people don't seem to realize is that, if there are mistakes in the way that you market your own business, many potential customers will conclude that they should not bother to do business with you. They will automatically assume that what you offer will be as shoddy as your marketing materials, and, of course, they may be right. This is not an image you want to convey.

When you are describing your business, don't tell people that you haven't really made your mind up about what you want to do, or that you are 'just giving it a go to see what happens'. If you are indecisive about your own concern, you may well unwittingly give the impression that you will be indecisive or unreliable when dealing with your customers. And why would anyone want to do business with someone who has already said that they might not be around for very long? Customers are much more likely to be loyal to businesses that are reliable and consistent in their own right.

7 Get connected

Computers are an essential element of almost every business. They are not there to ruin your life, but to make it easier. If the nature of your business is particularly artistic, or if you simply don't like computers, then you may find the whole area quite daunting. But it is essential that you get your act together at the outset otherwise you will have real problems later.

You will certainly need to buy a computer, and you may well want to consider a hand-held personal organizer to complement your mobile phone. That's really all you need to be efficient and professional. Carry the personal organizer at all times so that you can give instant responses about your availability. Don't say: 'I'll get back to you.' Tell them immediately when you can meet or complete some work, and agree it on the spot. This is an essential self-employed version of the 'Think Do' management principle in which you must do something the moment you think of it. The last thing you need when you run your own business is a list of people to get back to. Do it now. It saves doing everything twice, and it makes you seem really on the ball.

Put all your information on your personal organizer and computer, and back them up regularly on disk to avoid calamity (put these back-up reminders in your diary now). Think carefully about what you want your computer to do for your business, and choose your system accordingly.

- What information might you want to retrieve at some point in the future?
- What might your customers want to know?
- What might you want to know?
- What about your accountant or the dreaded tax inspector?
- What is the best way of cataloguing your records?
- What is the simplest way of doing all this?

Do not design your system around what the technology can do. Instead, decide what you want, and design something around those needs. Some careful thought at this stage could save you hours of heartache in the future.

8 Appoint a good accountant

There are whole books on this one subject, but let's stick to the basics. You really do need to know how to arrange all your financial affairs from the beginning. You won't want to discover at the end of the year that you have been recording information in the wrong way and that you now have to reorganize everything. Decide what you need, and organize all your money matters in the easiest possible way. Meeting your accountant once a year should be sufficient, with a few telephone calls every now and then to clarify any details. Keep it simple and think ahead. If you have money problems looming, address them early. Never succumb to the terrible practice of shoving bills in a problem drawer and ignoring them for months – you will create mounting debt and establish a reputation for not paying your suppliers. This is the slippery slope to bankruptcy.

Depending on the nature of your business, here are some of the gritty financial issues that must be addressed right at the beginning.

- Will you be a sole trader or will you register as a company at Companies House?

- Do you need separate bank accounts?
- If so, how many?
- How will your tax affairs be arranged?
- What type of National Insurance will you have to pay?
- Which elements of the business need to be kept financially separate?
- Do you need to rearrange parts of your current personal money habits to adjust to the new set-up?
- Do you need to register for VAT (value added tax)?
- What is the optimum system for paying the lowest amount of tax?

These fundamental questions need to be answered straightaway. Lots of people who work for themselves have started their first year without paying enough attention to these financial basics. At the end of their first trading year, they are then confronted by a nightmare of interrelated money matters that either cannot be undone, or cost a lot to disentangle. It is worth putting the work in now to avoid disappointment and unnecessary work in a year's time. There are many books on how to approach the technical detail, but the best thing to do is to have a frank meeting with the people who know about these things and then do exactly what they recommend before you start to generate any income.

9 Work out the materials you need

You need to work out precisely what materials you need to run your business. This sounds rather basic but you would be surprised by the number of people who drift into their new solo life without really knuckling down to resolve such basic questions as:

- If you are running a retail outlet, what stock do you need?
- How much investment does that involve?
- How quickly can you re-order?
- Do you know where from?
- Do you have the contacts?
- Where will stock be stored?
- Is it safe and secure?
- Is it insured?
- What system will you have for knowing when you are running out of stock?
- Are there legal requirements that you need to take into account?

If you are selling a service, at minimum you will need a clear description of what you are offering cogently written down. This might be a brochure, your CV, a client list, some examples of your skills, and a list of things that could be of interest to a potential customer. You will certainly need terms of business. Most businesses start without these, and only draw some up after their first debt. The smart person has them from the beginning to set a precedent and to head off financial problems from the off.

We will look at some of the most important general business tools in Chapter 3 ('Getting the money right'), but there may be some specific to your line of work that you can work out for yourself. Here is a basic checklist:

- Description of your business
- Your CV
- Your clients
- Examples of what you offer
- Examples of what you have done for others
- Prices
- Terms of business.

Whatever they are, get them organized now.

10 Network constantly without being irritating

What's the difference between networking and marketing? Not that much. As a start-up business, you are unlikely to have the funds to pay for an advertising campaign or other publicity. The main burden of letting people know that you are open for business falls on you. Thus, you need to overcome any shyness or reservations you may have about marketing your business.

Have business cards on you all the time, including during social time. This is where you will pick up lots of your work. Once you start chatting, most people are interested in what you do. Without forcing your product or service on them, you can always seem professional by letting them know what you offer and having your contact details to hand. There is a huge difference between basic marketing and being irritating. Calm, professional marketers state what they do in a clear, charming way. If the reaction of the other person is reasonably positive, they might hand over a card. It's amazing how, months later, the phone can ring and a potential new customer says 'I met you once and now I have a need for what you do ...'

This is a vital hurdle to overcome, particularly if you have a shy or reticent nature. Who do you think will be the better client? The one you cold-called and had a rather earnest meeting with? Or the one you met socially who decides to give you business in their own time? Speculative business meetings are no more scientific than interviews. They are based mainly on intuition. Yet if you already know you can get on socially with someone, or that they have a little insight into your private life, the chemistry part of the equation is already in place.

11 Now make it happen

You are now as ready as you will ever be to start your new working life. Take a little pause and reflect on all the elements you have organized:

- Have you thought of everything?
- Have you been rigorous with the issues?
- Have you been completely honest with yourself? (If the answer is no, you need to have a serious word with yourself because you cannot run your own business if you delude yourself.)

Do you have the energy and determination to see this thing through? (Bear in mind that you may need more resourcefulness than you think because there will always be something that you haven't thought of to trip you up.)

It is also very important to remember that, if *you* don't do it, it won't get done. Sitting around doing endless Venn diagrams and spreadsheets won't pay the bills. Ideas that work in theory but not in practice are not worth pursuing when you work on your own. Time is money. It's down to you and you alone. Scary? Certainly. Exciting? Absolutely.

So if you really want an answer to the question 'Where do I start?' the answer is: 'Right here, right now'.

Success Story: Dave Docherty, Hairdresser

Dave was a talented guy. He had lots of creative flair and decided to leave his big-name salon and set up his own shop. It would give him more freedom, and no one would be taking a cut of his fees. He didn't just dive in to his local high street and grab the nearest vacant premises. He researched his market thoroughly, searching out the competition and working out what he could offer that was more distinctive and had a sufficient catchment area.

He didn't make overblown assumptions about his income in the early days. He knew it would take a while to build up his clientele, so he factored that in and cut his cloth accordingly. He wrote a simple plan and explained it clearly to the bank so that they would understand his situation and stay off his back until things were well underway. In return, he sensibly did not waste capital on unrealistic items that had dubious potential for delivering a return on investment.

Dave got the right experts in place and set about creating a really distinctive identity for his shop and all his marketing materials. By pulling in a few favours and applying a fair amount of his own creative flair, he managed to produce all his initial marketing material for less than £500. By month four, he could already prove that they had paid for themselves. Dave had started well.

Chapter 1 Where do I start?
Checklist: what have you done? ✓

1 Assumed that you have something to offer ☐

2 Been honest with yourself ☐

3 Researched your market thoroughly ☐

4 Worked out how much money you need ☐

5 Written a simple, realistic plan ☐

6 Invested in a distinctive identity ☐

7 Got connected ☐

8 Appointed a good accountant ☐

9 Worked out the materials you need ☐

10 Networked constantly without being irritating ☐

11 Made it happen ☐

02

the right tools
for the job

In this chapter you will learn
- how to design your contact
  list
- how to design your new
  business hit list
- about keeping the numbers
  manageable
- how to work out what ratio
  of meetings generates how
  much work
- the importance of doing
  things when you think of
  them

It would be impossible for one book to cover every thing that every business needs to get launched. However, we can certainly put some essentials in place. At base level, it will be *you* who instinctively knows what you need in order to start your business, that is to say the tangible items such as systems, stock, premises, materials, and so on. With a little thought you can work out your computer software, how often you review the essentials, when to have meetings with your suppliers and business associates, and so forth. What you may not have considered in such detail are the less tangible items – the approaches and disciplines that you need to motivate yourself to get things done.

It is very much a theme of this book that, the simpler things are, the better they work. So in defining the right tools for the job, no attempt is made to persuade you to embark on any complicated systems or processes. In fact, the more complicated a system is, the less likely you are to get the job done. Here are the three sure-fire elements you need in order to generate a pipeline of initial business that will get you successfully launched, and enable you to keep business coming in when you have so much else to do all day.

These three really important tools will make your business a success:

Your most important tools

1 The contact list
2 The new business hit list
3 The telephone.

That's it. This is deliberately minimalist so there is no chance of you being distracted by massive spreadsheets with endless data on them. You don't want anything in the mix that wastes your time. There are many business people, and indeed consultants, who will try to convince you that you need various complicated systems to fuel your business plan. Experience suggests otherwise. The more paperwork and databases you have, the more confusion you have in the way of getting the job done. Some people love to hide behind this sort of stuff, but it doesn't work. The size of your database doesn't matter. The number of hot leads does. Piles of printouts don't matter. Two or three well-executed phone calls do. Consequently, we are going to look at these three elements and have a go at getting them under way.

12 Write out your contact list and new business hit list

The contact list

- The contact list is your lifeblood, and should be examined almost every working day.
- Start the first draft of the list by writing down everyone you know with whom you could possibly do business, and with whom you could get in touch.
- Ideally, it should only have the name of the person, the company and the date you last made contact with them on it.
- Don't be tempted to add other information. It will only distract you from the simple matter of picking up the telephone.
- If you really do feel that you need more information, write it somewhere else. Do not be tempted to enhance the list with extraneous detail – it has no bearing on the likelihood of you making the call, organizing a meeting, or achieving the thing that needs to be done, it only blurs your ability to get on with the task in hand.
- Every time you speak to someone or meet up with them, write the date down and move their details to the top of the list.
- This becomes your ready-made recall system. When you do not have anything to do, look at the very bottom of the list to see who you haven't been in touch with for some time (see Chapter 7, 'Have reserve plans for every day, p.92).
- Having this list basically means that you can never legitimately claim that you have nothing to do. If you ever actually find yourself believing that this is the case (very unlikely when you work on your own, but let's just suspend disbelief for the moment), then you simply go to the bottom of your contact list and call that person for a catch-up.
- If you fix a meeting or do get work as a result of that call, you might give yourself the afternoon off. That's down to you, because only you know whether you deserve it.

1 July

MEETINGS

Roger Hughes	Hughes & Taylor	Meet 9 Jul
Matt Nicholls	Kaleidoscope	Meet 10 Jul
Sarah Taylor	Cool Corporation	Meet 15 Jul

DONE

Julie Manders	BFJW	Met 30 Jun
Andy Vines	Z Consortium	Spoke 28 Jun
Dave Jones	Zing Agency	Met 22 Jun

PESTER LINE

Rachel Davis	Major Management	Spoke 23 May
Dave Bryanston	Ball & Associates	Met 6 May

Example contact list

- After some months have elapsed, draw a Pester Line at a certain date when you believe it is appropriate to call the client again. If you call more than once a month, you are probably pestering, but the appropriate frequency will depend on the nature of your business. Every six months is likely to be ideal in a service business where you are involved in one or two projects a year. But if you leave it a year, many of them will have left the company or changed their job description. Work out a frequency of contact that suits the nature of your business, and adjust it if it doesn't seem to be working.

When you call a client, always say when you last spoke or met. They will be impressed by your efficiency (see Chapter 6, 'Understanding time'). If you have judged the frequency right, the most likely reaction will be 'Wow, was it that long ago?' This proves that your call is timely, that it is not pestering, and that it represents an appropriate 'keep in touch' exercise.

If the client says call back on a certain date, then write the date in your personal organizer immediately, and then do it exactly when you said you would. This level of efficiency confirms that, if you do end up working for them, you will definitely deliver what you say.

The number of people on your contact list needs constant scrutiny. If there are more than 500 on the list at the outset, you are either fooling yourself or spreading yourself too thinly. It is much better to have a smaller number of viable, genuine prospects than a huge list full of people you don't really know.

Keep a constant eye on your frequency of contact. If you overdo it, after a period of receiving your (perhaps unwanted) solicitations, you will begin to tarnish your reputation (in other words, you will have overstepped the Pester Line). Or you will simply dissipate too much of your time on people who aren't interested in what you have to offer.

On the other hand, if there are less than 100 contacts on the list at the outset, your business may not be viable. If you were honest with yourself in Chapter 1, then you should have judged this correctly. You need a decent universe against which to apply the normal laws of probability. If you are utterly charmed, it is possible that you could sustain a living on five customers who give you precisely the amount of work that you want exactly when you need it. That's very unlikely, although it might just be feasible in a service industry where you have an established reputation that provides a ready-made flow of work.

Much more likely is a selection of potential clients who don't actually give you work despite regular promises; work which does eventually arrive but much later than you expected; projects which turn out to be much smaller than anticipated when they do eventually arrive; and so on. If you sell a product, you may to a certain degree be at the whim of various market forces, a series of random factors, and the possible effectiveness of whatever offers and promotions you decide to run. Therefore, it is better if you can generate your own pipeline to even out all these variations.

In the start-up phase of a service business, you are allowed to have only 50 contacts, but you will definitely need 100 within three months (see Chapter 6, 'Understanding time'). It is also worth considering whether your founder customers will continue to be long-standing customers and, if so, for how long. You will soon conclude that some will fall away, leaving the onus on you to develop fresh contacts. Be careful to consider this issue early, otherwise by the time you spot it in the normal run of things, you will already need the new work, and you will be dismayed by the time lag until new work materializes (see Chapter 6, 'Understanding time').

One of the most common laments of people working on their own is 'I'm too busy servicing existing customers to find new ones.' What feels like only moments later, the existing customers have moved on, and that person may well be out of business. Under no circumstances let this happen to you. It is your responsibility to become adept at running existing relationships whilst simultaneously engineering new ones. You are a plate spinner, a dextrous juggler, and a one-man band all rolled into one.

Scary but true: If you cannot generate 50 genuine contacts in the start-up phase of a service business, you should not be working on your own.

The new business hit list

Your second essential tool is the new business hit list. This is the list that you generate once your contact list has taken shape. You need to think carefully and very broadly about anyone who could have a bearing on the success of your business. This is not a cynical exercise in exploitation. It is merely casting the net as wide as possible to make the most of the potential contacts that you have.

13 Write down everyone you want to get in touch with

Take your time. This list will not appear as if by magic. You need to rack your brains a bit.

- Don't think only of the one person you know at a company
- What about colleagues, bosses and assistants?
- Would approaching several be more advantageous than only one?
- Have you considered friends with interesting jobs?
- Have you reviewed categories where you have related experience?
- Have you scoured the trade press?
- Have you remembered all your past colleagues who have moved on to other things?
- Think a long way back (you may surprise yourself)
- Have you included those who are still at your former places of work?

- As a rule of thumb, the majority of people on this list should be people that you do not know, whereas by definition those on the contact list will be known to you, if only initially via a phone conversation.

14 Put the phone number by every one of your contacts

This may sound pedantic but human nature will dictate that if the phone number isn't by the name, it simply gives you another excuse not to make the call. You will soon realize that, when you work for yourself, making excuses is the highest form of personal insult. You are basically saying that you are happy to let yourself get away with it. Well don't! If the number is by the name, you have no excuse. Now make the calls (see Chapter 5, 'Taming the telephone').

15 Do everything when you think of it, otherwise nothing will happen

This is another fantastic truism, but it really does work. Think about it. Things either are or they aren't. Have you made the call or not? When you think of something, then do it immediately. 'Think Do' is one of the most fundamental principles of the successful businessperson. Of course, you cannot do literally everything at once, but what you can do is write down everything that needs doing in a sensible order and work your way through it. The great advantage that you have here is that in an office other members of staff keep interrupting you. If you are on your own, these interruptions are far less frequent so you can get a great deal more done. Ten phone calls in less than an hour? No problem.

NAME	COMPANY	LAST SPOKE	NUMBER
PRIORITY			
Dave Jenks	Zebra	11 Oct	7234 0001
Sarah Bowen	HHZ	24 Oct	7654 9870
Richard Stokes	Fruit!	31 Oct	7222 0987
NEXT UP			
Roger Batty	RB Cleaners	10 Aug	8675 4321
Bob Hatton	Standard	8 July	8970 5647
Mary Brooks	Dragon Design	1 June	7664 7865

Example new business hit list

16 Constantly review the new business hit list to see if you are being realistic

There is no merit in generating a vast list of prospects to call only to make yourself feel good when, in truth, you are unlikely to get round to calling them all, or might not get through to many of them, let alone get work as a result. Refine your thinking regularly by asking direct questions:

- Where are you likely to have most success?
- Why is a certain approach not working?
- What new approach might work?
- How can you apply one set of skills to another market?
- Have you overlooked an obvious source of business?
- What type of work do you enjoy most?
- Where do you make the best margin?
- Which examples of previous work are most impressive?

Now start getting the list into some sort of priority order. Put the hottest prospects at the top and revise the order when things change.

17 Keep the numbers manageable

Any less than ten numbers on your hit list and you are being lazy. How long does it take to make ten phone calls? Less than an hour, which of course means that you cannot claim that you don't have the time. Any more than 50 and you will faze yourself and do nothing, rather like facing a plate with too much food on it. If you have trouble tackling a list of this size, break it down into manageable chunks that suit you. Groups of six or ten perhaps. Try colour-coding them so that you can distinguish one set from the other.

And if your first system doesn't work, simply admit it and invent a new one. Remember, any system is entirely for your own convenience and you don't have to discuss it with anyone else. Just make it work for you.

18 Keep inventing new ideas for contacting someone

You need to be vigilant about issues and trends. Pick up on articles in the trade press. Track movements of people and ideas. It works well when you ring up and say that you have noticed something relevant to them and have a suggestion. It shows that you are on the ball, and makes it easier to get work.

If you are selling products, keep re-analysing their appeal to your customer base.

- What is 'in' at the moment?
- Do your products fit that mood?
- Can you extend your range?
- What if you run a promotion?
- What if you alter your pricing?
- How about some local marketing?
- Are your marketing materials out of date or looking a little tired?
- Are there any seasonal events that you should be capitalizing on?

19 Every time you get through to someone, move them to your contact list

The definition of a contact is a meeting or a proper phone conversation. At bare minimum you will have explained who you are, provided your details and discussed the possibility of work at some point in the future. Never have someone on your contact list who should be on your new business hit list. This would be deluding yourself. They are not a genuine contact until you have spoken to them properly or met them and discussed at least the vague possibility of working together at some point in the future.

20 Try to have 20–30 meetings fixed for the next 4–6 weeks

In the early days, you need to pull out all the stops to generate some critical mass. That means a lot of meetings and probably a lot of coffee. Keep the meetings short and get to the point. You are a busy person and so are they. Never book more than four half-hour meetings in a day. You will lose energy and become bored of describing what you do. Two a day is ideal. Later on, when you have some paying customers, you can reduce this number and be more choosy. But to start with, there is no substitute for putting in the hard work.

The mathematics of this is discussed in more detail in Chapter 5, 'Taming the telephone', but the basics are as follows:

- The amount of business you think you currently have probably won't be enough
- Something unexpected will happen, so you need contingency income
- The law of averages will ensure that you will only get a percentage of the business you are aiming for
- So you need to work out your strike rate
- The number of contacts you need in order to fuel your business will be significantly greater than the number of customers or projects that you actually need to run a viable business
- You have to overcompensate, particularly in the start-up phase.

21 Never cancel a new business meeting because you are 'too busy'

'I'm sorry, I can't make it because I have too much on.'

This is a classic mistake that many people make. If you think about it carefully, you will realize that the person you are talking to could make a number of assumptions. If you are incredibly lucky, they will be impressed that you are so much in demand. But the more likely reaction is that you are a one-man band who is unable to cope. Which means that you certainly won't be able to handle whatever they might have in mind. Goodbye project! You may never get the meeting again, so you should say yes, and work harder for a brief period.

The telephone

The telephone is the third essential string to your bow, and we are going to get to grips with it in Chapter 5 ('Taming the telephone'). If you have a particular issue with 'cold-calling' or any other aspect of phoning people, you might want to read that chapter now. If not, don't worry for the moment. It's not nearly as daunting as you may think. Meanwhile, assuming that you have successfully established your two lists, you have the right tools for the job and you are ready to do business.

Cautionary Tale: Deborah Smith, Financial Consultant

Deborah thought she had it all sorted, but she didn't. She left the comfort of a financial firm with a hundred staff, and tried to run her new solo consultancy as though she still had the support systems of her old company. In big companies, other people always have spare copies of things, they do the status reports, and they remind you what you have to do, and when.

Deborah wasn't one for writing much down, so she didn't set up any contact or new business hit lists – she just allowed a random pattern of requests, meetings and calls to take on a life of their own. She managed to secure one job quite early on, which gave her the (ultimately false) impression that this 'working on your own' business would be fairly easy.

Lulled into a sense of security by her early lucky strike, she did not set aside any time to tee up any business for the months to come. By the time that first job was complete, she had nothing to do, and nothing in the pipeline. She had even committed the cardinal sin during her busy early phase of declining a new business meeting. When she rang the prospect back two months later, the need for her services had passed, and the feedback from the potential client was that they had been disappointed by what they regarded as a lack of enthusiasm and flexibility on her part.

After another three months of floundering around, Deborah took another salaried job in a large financial institution.

Chapter 2 The rights tools for the job

Checklist: what have you done? ✓

1 Written out your contact list and new business hit list ☐

2 Written down everyone you want to get in touch with ☐

3 Put the phone number by every one of them ☐

4 Done everything when you thought of it ☐

5 Constantly reviewed the list to see if you are being realistic ☐

6 Kept the numbers manageable ☐

7 Kept inventing new ideas for contacting someone ☐

8 Every time you got through to someone, you moved them to your contact list ☐

9 Tried to have 20–30 meetings fixed for the next 4–6 weeks ☐

10 Never cancelled a new business meeting because you are 'too busy' ☐

03

getting the money right

In this chapter you will learn
- how to concentrate on the money, but not become obsessed with it
- how to weigh up the service vs product distinction
- about the lucky seven money questions
- how to work out the price–quality equation
- about everyday flexible pricing

Whatever you do to make a living, and no matter how much you absolutely love it, there is no point in doing it unless you make a sensible amount of money for the effort you put in. You really owe it to yourself to get the money side of things right. So how exactly do we set about doing that?

22 Concentrate on the money, but don't become obsessed with it

The dreaded money. The filthy lucre. Yes, it's true. From now on, when you discuss money, it will be not in some abstract way based on a remote budget that was agreed by someone you have never met. It will be a highly personal matter. Have you ever noticed how company people talk about budgets, allocations and fiscals? They often adopt a rather blasé manner. They even say 'ten k' instead of 10,000! Once you have earned £10,000 entirely off your own bat, it is extremely unlikely that you will ever use the letter 'k' in that way again.

From now on, every time you discuss money it will all be your personal money, so you'd better start concentrating harder. It has been said that you don't really appreciate what running your own business means until you have experienced a bad debt, so it is essential that you become comfortable talking about money straightaway. If you don't, you will probably agree to produce unspecified amounts of work over unclear time periods, and in some instances you might not get paid at all.

Alternatively, you may consistently sell products at margins so low that your business will not be viable. Although this sounds incredibly obvious, huge numbers of businesspeople pursue a large volume of sales so that they can brag about the scale of their operation. They crow about turnover, but frequently they are barely making a profit. There is no merit whatsoever in rushing around all year creating things to do when you aren't actually making money. It doesn't make any sense. Therefore, address this by keeping a very close eye on your margin, and by constantly questioning *why* you are doing what you are doing (see Chapter 7, 'Never do anything unless you know why you are doing it', p.91).

23 Weigh up the service vs product distinction

It is extremely difficult to give general guidelines about how to handle money without distinguishing between service- and product-based businesses. If you produce or sell any form of product, then the basic equation of your business will be based on the cost of making or acquiring it in relation to the amount for which you sell it. That's your margin, or, put another way, 'materials with mark-up'. These businesses are almost always less profitable than service businesses that can attribute an acceptable price for an idea or a thing done (unless the manufacturer of that product has such enormous economies of scale that the amount of cash coming in makes the point irrelevant).

Of course this is a sweeping generalization, but it stands to reason that it is usually easier for a potential customer to attribute a perceived value to a tangible item than it is to an intangible one. Moreover, services and ideas can often cost nothing other than your time and talent to create. Consequently, in theory the price of a service or idea is limitless, whereas that of an item probably has a limit beyond which the market is unlikely to go. Consider this principle in relation to your own business. Ask yourself:

- What level of mark-up will your customers accept?
- What can you do to make what you provide worth more?
- Do you have enough services on offer to increase your average margin?
- Is your pricing appropriate for what you provide?

24 Work out how to have a near-infinite margin

If you run a service business, you should consider resisting the temptation to have offices, a partner, a secretary, and any other baggage. You may be able to operate without them. Before you tear off and spend a fortune on things that you may not actually need, look at these questions.

25 Consider the lucky seven money questions

The lucky seven money questions

1 Could you do without offices by working from home? ☐
2 If you cannot work from home, is there an elegant alternative? ☐
3 Could you operate without a formal business partner? ☐
4 Could you have less prescribed arrangements where you can bring contacts in as and when work dictates? ☐
5 Could you survive without delegating anything? ☐
6 With a little ingenuity and re-engineering, could you do everything you need yourself? ☐
7 Could you pay yourself less for a while? ☐

If the answer is yes to all of these, you can have a near-infinite margin. Of course, there are always those who claim that the sociability and interaction provided by an office environment are essential to the way they work. Fair enough. But you can imitate the important elements of these circumstances in almost every way by having plenty of meetings, bouncing ideas off friends, and having a decent social life. In fact, being self-employed should massively improve your social reliability. For once in your life, you have no silly commute and no boss forcing you to stay at the office, so you can have much more enterprising free time on your own terms. You will probably live longer and have fewer medical bills as well.

26 Try to avoid the most time-consuming business issue ever: other people

Ever heard of 'high maintenance' members of staff? This is because one of the most time-consuming issues in any business is other people. No one is suggesting that you become a hermit, and perhaps your business genuinely cannot function without a workforce. However, if you are working for yourself, you do at least have the option to consider structuring a business that minimizes the effect others can have on your fortunes. You owe it to yourself to consider whether there is any possibility that you *could* run your business without anyone else. If there is any chance that you might, it is a strongly recommended option. Why? Because when you are on your own you:

- Make clearer decisions
- Make faster decisions
- Do business in your own unique style
- Avoid having to deal with politics
- Do not have to feel guilty about relationships with colleagues
- Can experience a truly direct link between effort and reward.

27 Try to sell what you do, not materials with a mark-up

There are many other things that can make an enormous difference to your profitability. Your talents theoretically have a limitless price. That means that, within certain sensible parameters, you can charge what you want. Materials are finite and have an approximate known price, so they can usually be undercut by a competitor and thus decrease your margin. The smartest sole traders do not sell materials or any fixed price service. They sell experience and ideas. This is not a way to rip off customers – quite the opposite. The most powerful question you can ask is:

'If I fix x, what is it worth to your business?'

The answer to this question is quite fascinating. Some potential customers will not have the foresight to estimate (or, in their eyes, speculate wildly) what they might gain by engaging your services. In which case, they won't answer the question or will not be prepared to say that the answer might be quite a large figure. This means that they are either not a genuine potential customer or that they will be a penny-pinching bad one, which means that you should not be pursuing their business anyway.

An enlightened potential customer will rapidly be able to put a likely figure on what they stand to gain (or not lose) from your involvement, and they will be big enough to tell you the true amount. Once you get into honest conversations of this type, you can forge a direct link between your price and the customer benefit. After a number of similar conversations, you may well have enough evidence and confidence to double your prices.

28 The price–quality equation: if you cost a lot, you must be good

What do you deduce about two products of similar type, one of which costs £2,000 and the other £200? The more expensive is probably better made and so of higher quality. It may have a cachet or brand value to which potential buyers aspire. There is nothing wrong with it being more expensive, assuming that there are people who appreciate those qualities and are prepared to pay for it. No matter how disparaging one chooses to be about products and services that are 'expensive', one is eventually forced to admit that, one way or another, there must be a market for them otherwise they would not remain in their market.

In which case, what would you deduce about two people, one of whom commands a fee of £2,000 a day, and the other £200? The more expensive is likely to be more experienced and therefore of higher quality. This is self-fulfilling, because if they are not, then in a fairly short space of time they will not generate any repeat business, and will fail as a business reasonably quickly.

It may be something of a rhetorical question, but which of these two people would you rather be? Obviously it is a hypothetical example and the gap between the two figures doesn't really matter, but the principle probably does. Far too many people who work on their own undercharge for their services, and it is often a mystery why. Nervousness certainly plays a part. Lack of confidence contributes too. And many will claim that if they put their prices up, they will either lose or fail to gain work. But if you think it through carefully, you will pretty much always look enviously upon someone who is successful in a particular field and come to the following conclusion:

If they cost a lot, then they must be good.

This is, of course, the reaction that you should aspire to invoke in your customers and competitors. Clearly there has to be an appropriate balance between price and delivery but, in the main, you should always place the maximum possible value on what you have to offer. If you are uncertain about what that value is, you need to test your pricing first. One of the lovely things about being self-employed is that you can effectively reinvent yourself and what you offer every day. If yesterday's formula didn't work, try another today. Now consider putting your prices up, and be prepared to turn work down if customers want it too cheap. Your central maxim should be:

Charge a premium price and do a great job.

29 Aim for 50 per cent repeat business within three years

If this aim frightens you, there is something wrong with your ambitions. Do you expect your customers to be pleased with the work that you do? If the answer is yes, which it certainly should be, then you should expect further work in due course. If you are selling products, there is still a service element to what you do, and your objective must be to have your customers coming back. Even accounting for the random availability of projects, seasonal factors and the cyclical nature of certain markets, you should always aspire to get more business from at least half of your existing customers.

You should also track satisfied customers when they move house, move to new jobs or have a change of circumstances. Whatever has happened, they will be confronted by a whole new set of issues, many of which you may be able to address. In a service business in particular, it is important to go and have a coffee with people when they move. It is flattering for them, it gives you a flavour of their new set-up, and there is always something new to discuss.

Of course aiming for 50 per cent could be criticized as banal. Who in their right mind would aim for a percentage? It is merely a figure that will fluctuate anyway depending on the size and shape of the other elements in your business. What should make sense though are the parameters above and below which repeat purchase levels should not rise or fall. If you have 100 per cent repeat business, then the corollary is that you have no new business. This is not good. If you have no repeat business, then you would certainly be worried about the quality and value of what you produce and the long-term prospects for your business, if only judged by word of mouth recommendation and customer satisfaction. And if you had a fantastic run of new business, then you would not mind at all if your repeat percentage fell. Perhaps we should conclude that the percentage should be no lower than 30 per cent and no higher than 70 per cent in any given year.

30 Don't be small-minded about money

Think big. Remember that you will probably have to type all your own invoices and do your own VAT return, so don't waste time with bits and pieces that don't get you anywhere. When quoting and invoicing, stick to units of hundreds or thousands of pounds. It is difficult to generalize here, but the basic rule is not to mess about with small fractions that do not really add to your profit, but which infuriate you when doing the books. Keep it simple and round the figures up or down (preferably up) in order to get the job done quickly and efficiently. In some instances you may lose a little on price, and in others you may gain a little, but you will save hours of fiddling about with pounds and pence or dollars and cents.

This is an extension of the 'successful people buy in bulk' principle, and applies to anyone who works on their own. Successful business people buy in bulk so that they don't have to waste time perpetually buying individual small units of a given item. This applies to pretty much everything: paper, paper clips, printer cartridges, stamps, envelopes – that rather irritating list of stuff which has to be done but doesn't really seem to have a bearing on anything. Time-wasters (who are never successful working on their own) repeat the process mindlessly again and again, usually failing to notice that the time spent on constantly doing this is detracting from their ability to do much more rewarding and profitable things. Put another way: have you heard the one about the person who never got anything done because they kept writing out lists of 'Things to do'?

Expenses are a case in point. No matter what your business, do not be petty about expenses. If at all possible, you should never charge them to the customer. If appropriate, build a suitable margin into your prices to allow for any extra services that you would normally wish to provide them. In a service business, be generous and broad-minded. Buy the client lunch, and pay for your own travel. Simply get on with it in a way that befits a well-paid successful person.

There are plenty of examples in Chapter 7, 'How to conduct yourself', that give suggestions to help you along, but here is just one example. If you find yourself producing estimates for jobs that go into tiny detail and try to justify your every movement, you have probably either got the wrong pricing or the wrong type of customer. What a lot of people who work for themselves forget is that discussing the trivia takes as much time as talking about the important things. It therefore costs just as much money, but as a proportion of the value of the lower priced job, the time spent will probably not be viable. Therefore, be very careful not to become dragged into the mire of discussing tiny financial details whilst all the time you are missing the main point. If a customer becomes too uptight about a job and will not agree what you deem to be a fair and honest price for a job well done, walk away from the job. You are better than that.

Furthermore, don't forget that your accountant can make allowances for all sorts of things, and tidy up all the details at the end of the year. That's what you pay them for.

31 Be canny about requests for free or 'win only' work

'Share in our success or failure' was one of the worst traits of the dot com boom in the late 1990s. This is a euphemism for 'I won't pay for anything unless things have gone really well and I decide that I can afford it.' The main rule is never to give anything away for free, unless you have an overwhelming reason to. When people ask why you won't do speculative work, the best answer is 'Because I don't need to'. They really have no response to that.

Although there is usually no reason to give your time away for free, you do of course reserve the right to charge less or provide free work if you deem that it is appropriate. You should try not to, but you are the best judge of any given state of affairs, and the joy of working on your own is that you do not have to discuss it with anyone else. Here are some possible reasons why you *might* want to provide something free or at a reduced price:

- Because it will lead to repeat business
- Because it will lead to new business
- Because it is part of a much bigger deal
- Because they are a highly-valued customer
- Because you can.

A final thought on free work. If you have had a really good year, why not offer to work free for a charity or a worthy cause for a limited period? Your expertise may be worth significantly more than any donation you might ordinarily make, and skills are often more useful than cash. No money needs to change hands, and you can add their name to your client list and use it as part of your sales patter.

32 Consider everyday flexible pricing

Here's a slightly radical idea that is not for the faint-hearted: Everyday Flexible Pricing. Each day when you work on your own is effectively the beginning of a new financial year. You can state your prices any way you like, describe your background as you see fit, and accept or decline work on a whim. It really is entirely down to you. Which means you could double your prices tomorrow if you like.

This may or may not be a good idea in your market. However, you could certainly test two pricing levels side by side and see if it has any bearing on the success of a deal. Or you could steadily increase your prices as your confidence, experience and flow of work increases. For example, if you are discussing a project that is very similar to one you have just done, increase the price by as much as you think suits, probably somewhere between 10 and 50 per cent. If the client accepts, then this becomes your new price for an exercise of that type.

Over time, this should fuel an ever-upward value equation for your business. One word of warning though: if you do try this, make absolutely sure that you know which prices you have quoted, and to whom, otherwise you may lose the plot and come across as though you are making it up as you go along. Which, of course, would be the truth.

Success Story: Samantha Blades, Health Club Owner

Samantha built up her experience in a large chain of health clubs but never felt comfortable with their corporate strictures. As far as she was concerned, she would be able to run a much better operation given half the chance. She knew that club membership is subject to price barriers just like every other market, but felt that people would be prepared to pay a premium price for a truly personal and high-quality service that would contrast sharply with the cattle market approach of many of the large chains.

She invested in a luxurious environment, the very best products and, most importantly, she paid 25 per cent more than the competition for the best staff. Potential users of the club could tell straightaway that these were happy, knowledgeable, well-motivated people. She marketed heavily to the better-off end of the market and, sure enough, they were only too happy to pay a higher price for it.

Every now and then someone would ask for a discount. She always said no, unless there were exceptional circumstances such as a bulk corporate deal. But in other financial respects, she was extremely generous. She frequently provided free lunch for her customers, and bought them presents on their birthdays, which she had thoughtfully captured on her database.

She worked on the principle that if you cost a lot, you must be good. And she was.

Chapter 3 Getting the money right

Checklist: what have you done?   ✓

1 Concentrated on the money, but not become obsessed with it ☐

2 Weighed up the service vs product distinction ☐

3 Worked out how to have a near-infinite margin ☐

4 Considered the lucky seven money questions ☐

5 Tried to avoid the most time-consuming issue ever: other people ☐

6 Tried to sell what you do, rather than materials with a mark-up ☐

7 Examined the price–quality equation: If you cost a lot, you must be good ☐

8 Aimed for 50 per cent repeat business within three years ☐

9 Not been small-minded about money ☐

10 Been canny about requests for free or 'win only' work ☐

11 Considered everyday flexible pricing ☐

04

how to communicate effectively

In this chapter you will learn
- how to choose the right communication method
- to become adept at describing what you do in 30 seconds
- how to introduce some humanity into your CV
- why it is important to meet lots of people and to stay open-minded
- to pay attention to customers and ask them what they want

Communication. This must surely be one of the most complicated issues in life, let alone in a business context. Where would we be without communication? Humans cannot exist without it. Almost everything we do involves the need for it. And yet often we really aren't very good at it. So let's have a look at some of the methods at our disposal, and work out how best to use them.

33 Choose the right method of communicating

Methods of communicating are constantly changing. Up until relatively recently you could only really talk to someone in person, by telephone or by writing them a letter. That was about it. You might have faxed someone or sent a courier to speed things up a little. Then came the internet and mobile telephony, and the whole scene changed. We now require a much broader set of communication skills, and we need to put much more thought into what is the appropriate method for any particular situation. We can try to put these options into some sort of hierarchy. Here is a rank order of possible communication methods, based on (a) the likelihood of you being correctly understood and (b) probable sales success as a result:

1 Talking face to face
2 Telephone conversation
3 Letter
4 E-mail
5 Text message.

With regard to effectiveness, option number one must beat all the rest by a hundred to one. Consequently, if at all possible, only conduct your important business face to face. However, this is not an excuse for endorsing a 'meetings culture' in which legions of earnest businesspeople sit in meetings all day without really knowing why. Quite the opposite, in fact. It is perfectly feasible to conduct meetings in a brisk, polite way that acknowledges the fact that most people are busy. Come in, get to the point, agree what is to be done, and get out. Half an hour is the ideal length for a business meeting (have a look at Chapter 8, 'Meetings can be fun').

Having a good telephone conversation can also be highly productive. Nevertheless, there is a huge difference between a telephone conversation with someone that you have not met in person as opposed to one with someone whom you can picture. Everything is easier if you have met, so if it is important, make sure that you do indeed meet. Have a look at Chapter 5 ('Taming the telephone') for all sorts of ways to make your phone conversations more pleasant.

Letter writing is next down the list, but a very long way behind. In the direct marketing industry, the average response rate to letters is around 2 per cent. It wouldn't be much use if you only got through to two out of every 100 of your prospects, so letters have to serve a very distinct purpose. If you know that the recipient likes to have things written down, then a letter makes sense. If you have done a lot of research into the potential reader and you have a carefully-argued and quite bespoke proposal, then a letter may work, particularly if it is followed by an appropriately timed phone call.

And so we come to the dreaded e-mail. In many respects, this method has completely revolutionized our lives. Certainly, many people who work on their own could not succeed without it because of its fantastic ability to deliver things quickly and its power to enable them to stay in touch. The internet has also facilitated the transfer of much more information, and access to all sorts of data that would previously have been cumbersome and costly to obtain.

Yet as a high quality communication method, e-mail leaves much to be desired. Why? Because:

- Anything you send can be totally ignored
- The presentation style is mainly in the hands of the receiver, not you
- Most messages are not checked, so that any errors can make you look unprofessional or ignorant
- People you don't know about are sometimes blind copied on the original for political purposes that you know nothing about
- Your original message or reply is often forwarded to someone you know nothing about.

The sort of chaos that can ensue from these five possibilities shouldn't really require any further elaboration. Suffice to say that any communication method that has these pitfalls needs to be treated with extreme caution. It is perfectly fine to bat e-mails back and forth with a known customer who likes the method, but otherwise it is unlikely to be the method by which you grow your business. E-user beware!

34 Become adept at describing what you do in less than 30 seconds

Lethologica is an inability to recall words. This is not something that you would ever want to suffer from. Now that you work on your own you need to improve your word power so that you are very proficient at explaining what you do. Potential customers may be interested for a maximum of one minute. This is true at an interview, a drinks party, in the pub, at the squash club – anywhere in fact. After that, they become bored. You need to get your act together and come across in a lucid, enthusiastic way.

Start by writing down what you do in no more than three sentences. Now read it out loud. Does it sound daft? If so, rewrite it. Try again. Does it sound like a cliché? Does it sound like all the other waffle you read in corporate brochures or hear from politicians on the television? If so, change it. Make it fun and engaging. Do it with some pride and a lot of energy. Excellent. Now you can use it for face-to-face conversations, telephone calls and all your written work. Also bear in mind that this should evolve constantly to keep pace with the manner in which your business develops.

35 Be prepared to improvise on the spot

Life's a mess. Make it up as you go along! One of the joys of running your own business is that you can change the rules any time you like – several times a day if you are feeling particularly mischievous. There's nothing more boring than someone who repeats the company mantra in a soulless manner, so go with the flow a little. If you spot an opportunity, try out a sales angle. If you have a random thought, say it. If you want to discuss an idea without necessarily proposing it, then do so. It's vibrant and fun.

36 Introduce some humanity into your CV

You've all seen the type of thing:

'Relentlessly successful, moved from A to B to C, married with two children, enjoys theatre and music.'

That's the gist of the average CV. What can we deduce about this individual? Are they extremely reliable or just really boring? The best that we can guess is that they are a fairly steady individual. Let's compare them with the next one:

'Gained experience doing X, transferred skills to different industry Y, broke away and set up on own doing Z, plays in a rock band, flies birds of prey at the weekends, amateur artist and occasional cartoonist.'

Who would you prefer to have a drink with? Who would you rather do business with?

You get the idea. If you introduce some humanity into your business life, interesting things start to happen. First, you get to know your customers so much better, not because you are asking inane questions such as 'Did you have a good weekend?', but because you really get to know what they are up to, and in most cases people do some very interesting and enterprising things that they never mention unless you ask. Second, if you work in the type of business where it is appropriate to overlap your work and social life, the whole thing becomes a pleasure instead of a chore. Third, smart customers deduce very quickly that if you are enterprising in your spare time, you probably are in your working time as well. Finally, mentioning your hobbies and outside interests can give you that extra element of pride in your achievements that is crucial to anyone who works on their own. There's nothing wrong with drawing satisfaction from your hobbies as well as your work and transferring that confidence between the two whenever you need it.

37 Remember that people give business to those with whom they like having meetings

In Chapter 8 ('Meetings can be fun') we will discuss meetings in detail, but for the purposes of good communication you need to acknowledge what meetings are for in the first place:

- To establish a relationship
- To propose something
- To agree something.

That's about it really, and unless anything is incredibly complicated, you should be able to do what is necessary in less than an hour, and preferably less. If you are the sort of person who waffles, who has meetings without really knowing why, who doesn't prepare, and who fails to bring new ideas and proposals with them, you will be quite tedious to have meetings with. This is not a favourable impression to create. You need to be really on the ball. Don't set up meetings for the sake of it. Always ask yourself: 'What's the point?' Be sharp and lively, and establish a reputation as a person with whom a meeting is always a pleasure. You want your customers to be saying: 'Whenever I have a meeting with you I get something out of it.'

38 Meet lots of people and stay open-minded

Let's spend a moment or two discussing the difference between networking and meeting lots of people. Over time you can become quite good at working out the difference between the two. When you start out, you do actually need to meet quite a lot of people. This is because the law of averages proves that you need a reasonable critical mass of contacts to make any business work. In the early days, the shape of your business will not be sharply defined (no matter how rigorous you were in the planning stages), so you need to stay open-minded.

Moreover, bear in mind that every meeting you have involves a judgement of character as well as an assessment of someone's technical skills. The more people you communicate with, the more experience you will have of working out whether you will get on well with them, and whether they will be relevant to your aspirations for your business. Once you have met, you need to keep a close eye on what happens next. Try asking yourself these types of questions:

- Did they send through the thing that they said they would in the meeting?
- Did they call in two weeks' time as they promised?
- Did they give my details to their colleague as we agreed?
- Did they consider my proposal and give me a response?

If the answer to any of these is yes, you may be onto a decent working relationship. If the answer is mainly no, you need to consider carefully whether the person is a time-waster or someone who usually fails to do what they say they will. If this proves to be the case, they will not be fulfilling to do business with and, if they are an associate of any kind, be aware that their poor approach will reflect badly on you.

Once you have met a number of people, you can refine your approach into some proper networking. This is not a cynical process whereby you extract all the benefits from people and give them nothing back. In some quarters, the very word 'networking' has as bad a reputation as 'Sales'. Properly executed networking should benefit everyone. Let's define the difference between meeting many people and networking. In the early days, you need to meet lots of people and stay open-minded. When you have built up some experience of their capabilities and your aspirations, you can network. This will involve keeping in contact with those who could benefit from your skills and vice versa, at a frequency that is appropriate to your line of work and how busy they are. You keep in touch, help them out, suggest things and, ideally, do business together. Everyone wins.

39 Take your customers to lunch and insist on paying

It could be lunch. It could be breakfast, dinner, the races or even just a drink. The details don't matter. The thing is that social surroundings promote a totally different mood than those of a meeting room, many of which appear to be designed precisely to *reduce* the chances of meetings being enjoyable. Suggesting a social get-together is a constructive, magnanimous thing to do. What does it say about you? It says that:

- You are broad-minded
- You are interested in other aspects of your customers than their money
- You can afford it.

Therefore, you will be engineering a situation in which you can show your generosity, your interest in the client, and quite possibly the degree to which you are on the ball with your suggestions of places to go and things to do.

What do you talk about when you meet up? A bit of business, certainly. But mainly simply ask short, open-ended questions and then shut up. You'll be amazed what comes up. People will talk when they are put at ease. They will talk about their families and relationships, their concerns, their feelings about their job, sport, hobbies, current affairs – pretty much anything. Of course there are some bores in the world, but in the main there are interesting things to learn and discuss. The more ideas you have, the smarter you will appear, not because you are faking it but because it will be true. It's all part of honing good communication skills.

40 Rewrite all your marketing materials

Assuming that you do succeed in creating a dynamic environment for your business, things will probably change quite rapidly and so should the manner in which you describe what you do. The chances are that your marketing materials will become obsolete pretty quickly. So update them. It doesn't have to be an expensive exercise if you stick to the basics and concentrate on the elements that work well in your market.

Get out all the stuff that you have had done and spread it out on a large table. Ask yourself some questions:

- What do you think of the materials?
- Do they accurately represent what you do these days?
- Which bits worked and which didn't?
- What can you learn from that?
- Do you use some elements more than others?
- Has the emphasis of your business changed?
- Is there any point in producing something new?

41 Design a clever mailing to send to your customers

It's amazing the number of businesses that send out one launch mailing and then sit back thinking that they have 'done marketing'. Oh dear. The market is changing all the time. People come and go. Products and tastes change. You can never conclusively prove that something that didn't work before won't work now.

Consider the merits of sending out a new mailing to your customers:

- What would you say?
- Have you ever done it before?

- Did you learn anything?
- Who would you send it to?
  - Existing customers for repeat purchase?
  - Or new potential customers? If so, where will you get their details?

42 Ask your customers what else you could do for them

How many businesses plough on churning out the same old stuff, assuming that what they provide is what their customers want? Most people don't like change unless someone else does all the work and makes it a pleasure. Then they can opt in or out on their own whim and in their own time. Unfortunately, when you work on your own, that someone is you. It is your job to stay very close to your customers and the markets in which you operate.

When you have some new ideas that you want to test, or even if you have none at all (hopefully not, otherwise you may be lacking the entrepreneurial spirit shown by most people who work on their own), talk to your customers. Ask them:

- What else could I do for you?
- Did you realize that what I do for you is only a fraction of what I do for some of my other customers?
- How much does what I do make a difference to your business?
- What are the main things preoccupying you at the moment?
- Would you like me to investigate something new for you?
- Are you dissatisfied with any suppliers who provide similar services to me?
- Do you know any other potential customers who might want to use my services?
- What could I do better?

By now you will know that when you ask such open-ended questions, it is your job to shut up and pay attention. The new selling opportunities are always lurking in the answers given. Let the clients talk. In many instances, your customers will invent new work for you on the spot. Occasionally drop in new ideas. Offer to develop a thought into a proposal. Suggest that you do a little development work on a subject and call them next week to see if it is worth proceeding. In the modern business world they call this being *proactive*. In truth it is simply having ideas and getting things done.

Cautionary Tale: Richard Baker, Caterer

Richard could make really good sandwiches but was a bit limited when it came to good communication. His idea of marketing was to have a shop called The Sandwich Shop ('it does what it says on the tin', he used to joke to his mates), and his advertising campaigns consisted of a couple of hand-drawn cards in the window saying Sandwiches, Rolls, Salads.

He was an introverted sort of fellow, and the long hours demanded by the business (particularly the early starts for the bacon sandwich crowd on the way to work) meant he didn't get out and socialize much. So he never really increased his circle of friends and attracted new customers other than the standard passing trade.

He could have done so much more. He could have leafleted all the local businesses alerting them to the fact that he could do the catering for all their meetings. He could have had a discounted dish of the day. He could have set up a delivery service for local business people who never took lunch breaks. He could have let all his weekday customers know that he could cater for their weekend parties as well.

But he didn't, so he still sells cheese and tomato in the same quantity that he always did. Is there a Richard Baker in your High Street?

Chapter 4 How to communicate effectively

Checklist: what have you done?   ✓

1 Chosen the right method of communicating ☐

2 Become adept at describing what you do in less than 30 seconds ☐

3 Been prepared to improvise on the spot ☐

4 Introduced some humanity into your CV ☐

5 Remembered that people give business to those with whom they like having meetings ☐

6 Met lots of people and stayed open-minded ☐

7 Taken your customers to lunch and insisted on paying ☐

8 Rewritten all your marketing materials ☐

9 Designed a clever mailing to send to your customers ☐

10 Asked your customers what else you could do for them ☐

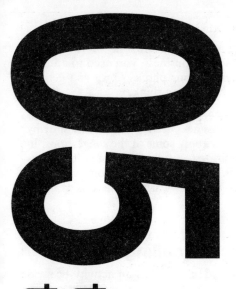

05

taming the telephone

In this chapter you will learn

- to overcome fears and prejudices about cold-calling
- how to understand the relationship between the number of calls and the eventual amount of work
- to prepare your selling angles
- a system for noting your calls
- the ten golden rules of unsolicited calling

The phone is a two-way machine that can be a great asset or an object that invokes considerable fear. Many people hate what they describe as 'cold-calling'. If you are one of them, and particularly if you are in a service business, you need to address this issue urgently and befriend your phone. Once you get the hang of it, it's really not as bad as you think.

With regard to the telephone, there are certain matters that anyone who runs their own business needs to confront. Start by reading this chapter and try to apply some of the suggestions. In particular you need to scrutinize carefully 'The ten golden rules of unsolicited calling', p.69. Whatever you do, don't reject the idea before you have a go – it is not nearly as onerous as many would have you believe.

43 Don't call it 'cold-calling'

Who said cold-calling was cold? Rarely has an activity been so badly titled. Calling someone on the phone is usually a very pleasant thing to do. Even in business. In reality, those who view it as cold-calling are probably cold themselves, and are not that keen on other people anyway. It is far better to view the whole process as just calling someone for a chat. The fact that you have never met that person has nothing to do with it. If you are charming and have something interesting to say, it will be a pleasure for both sides. You wouldn't hesitate to call a friend, and sometimes you might even call them without a reason. In business, there is always a reason, so all you have to do is state clearly what the reason is and get to the point.

There are many ideas here about how to get the conversation started and overcome the initial hurdles. However, they will work to a lesser degree until you get to grips with the emotional barriers and convince yourself that it really isn't such a big deal to pick up the phone, and that great things can happen once you take the plunge. One way to do this is to consider all the worst things that could possibly happen if things don't go as well as you hoped. Here are some examples:

They say they are not interested in what you do

So what? This is very valuable information. Lots of people spend weeks, months, years even, pursuing someone who simply isn't interested in what they have to offer, and never will be. This could be an individual or a company whose culture doesn't suit yours and vice versa. Take it on the chin and move on.

They refuse to take your call

This is most interesting. If someone spends the bulk of their time hiding behind a barrage of secretaries and assistants, there are two things you can deduce about them. Either they may be genuinely busy, or they enjoy creating the *impression* that they are busy. If it is the former, then it doesn't mean that they are not interested in what you do. Either keep trying or use a different method of getting in touch that suits their style better. If it is the latter, you need to think carefully about whether you would really like to do business with them. Will they be a badly-behaved customer? Will they respond to your calls if you do end up working together? Will they pay you on time? And there are a host of other issues that could make your life a misery. 'Only do business with people you like' is a maxim that will serve you well.

They are rude or dismissive

This is a bit unpleasant but no less helpful than either of the above. Rude people may well occupy influential positions for intermittent periods, but nobody enjoys working with them and, over time, the system spits them out. If you work on your own, there is absolutely no point in dealing with people of this type. They ruin your life and they do not deserve your contribution. Avoid them like the plague.

44 Admit that the phone will never ring unless you market yourself

Many people who set up on their own make the mistake of thinking that the phone will ring and provide them with work in the same way that it did when they were employed in a company. It doesn't. In fact, on some days, it doesn't ring at all. One or two extremely blessed individuals come out of corporate life and seem to have a charmed flow of ready-made work without appearing to have to market themselves. But one thing is for sure: it never lasts. In year two or three, these people are left adrift as that source of business fades.

Besides which, you may not even have a contact base from a former life. In this case, you need to market yourself from the outset, to a fairly broad audience. The first stepping stone in this process is admitting that the phone is unlikely to ring unless you make it do so. In other words, you need to create the momentum that makes people want to call you back, whether that is today or at some point in the future when they have a need for your product or service.

This is a very simple piece of logic. If you don't ask the girl out, she won't even know you are interested. If you don't call and express an interest, then potential customers won't consider you.

45 If you make 100 calls, you will get 40 meetings, and three jobs

The precise figures may vary depending on the nature of your business, but the essence of the equation never does. Take a moment to think about this. It stands to reason that you must generate a critical mass of interest in what you have to offer. The mathematics of it has nothing to do with the quality of you, your product or service, or your customer base. If you jot down all the possible reasons why someone does *not* want to do business with you this week, you will soon see how circumstances are more likely to stop work happening than to start it.

Start with these reasons why people will have no need for your services this week, and add your own:

- Holiday
- Illness
- Apathy
- Disorganization
- Budget change
- Colleague disagreeing
- Company politics
- A rival proposal
- Other priorities
- Haven't got round to it.

You could double the length of this list in less than a minute. That's without even entertaining genuine overriding business considerations such as price, quality, distribution, over-supplied markets, or product specification. Once you think about it, it's a miracle that anything ever gets done at all.

Remember: 100 calls = 40 meetings = three jobs

This is why people keep talking about the 'pipeline' in a new business context. In truth, it is more helpful to see it as a funnel or hopper. The work appears to come sequentially in a linear way, but actually it only appears to be that way because, at any given moment, you have many contacts and proposals which, in all probability, will generate work at some point, but not necessarily now. It never happens all at once, and that is precisely why you need a regular flow of people who just might be interested in your offer in any given week or month.

When you run your own business, the moment you believe that you have a settled and steady customer base, everything may well be about to go wrong. Why? Because you will have failed to prime your next source of business to replace the business that you will inevitably lose soon, based purely on the law of averages. Some people claim that they fail to do this because they are too busy. This is a very poor excuse, particularly when you consider the huge irony of having too much time on your hands when you have lost a significant customer.

Perhaps another reason for not preparing is that you don't think it will happen to you because your quality is high and your relationship with your customers is good. That may well be true, but it has almost nothing to do with whether you will retain them or not. At some point, the law of averages will cause some factor you had not considered to jeopardize your business.

It may not be 'your fault', but it will certainly be 'your problem', so anticipate it and fix it before it is irretrievably broken.

46 Prepare your selling angles

Now let's get down to the business of what you are actually going to say on the phone. You've done the hard part: you've sat down with a list of people to call, researched all their numbers (see Chapter 2), and you've dialled. So what exactly are you going to say? You need to consider some selling angles:

- Who are you?
- What do you do?
- Why are you calling?

- What do you (or your business) offer?
- What has it got to do with them?
- What do you want to happen next?
- What happens if they are not there and someone else answers?

You need to work through all these possibilities before you call. Don't dial and then panic. If you have considered all the angles beforehand, you won't be caught on the hop. Never leave a message. If you do, you immediately cede control of the contact to the other person. This means that, the moment you call again, you are pestering.

47 Don't use jargon to disguise what you do

So you have got through to the person you want to speak to. Stay calm. Remember that waffle and jargon are the last preserve of corporate behemoths. We all know that obscure phraseology is designed to confuse people so that it seems as though you need their services (and so that they can charge you more). But when you work on your own, the opposite is true. If they can't grasp what you do in one sentence, they won't bother to listen to the rest. Cut out the waffle and come straight to the point. If you are unfamiliar with the word 'obfuscation', look it up in the dictionary. It will say something like 'to make something unnecessarily difficult to understand'. This is the opposite of what you want to achieve.

Use clear, simple expressions to explain what you do and why you would like to do business with the potential client. Don't be vague about what you do – let them grasp it quickly and move the conversation on to the area that matters to you.

If you find this difficult, and you still sound vaguer than a vague thing, try some of these techniques:

- Pretend you are explaining it to your mother or father
- Phrase it as though you were talking to your mate in the pub
- Write it down and eliminate anything that sounds silly
- Say it out loud and ask yourself whether you sound daft
- Tape record it, listen back, and decide if you would welcome such a phone call
- Practise saying it in front of the mirror

- Try it on the phone, then debrief yourself as to whether you sounded sensible – if not, draw up a new version.

But whatever you do, make sure you do all this *before* you call. It really is essential that you sound lucid and persuasive, and under no circumstances use a vital prospect as a guinea pig for a ham-fisted dry run that goes wrong. Get organized in advance and get it right.

48 Tell them you are available

There is a tendency in modern business to create the impression that you are always frantically busy. This is completely inappropriate for someone who runs their own business. You need to strike the right balance. For a start, people soon detect whether you always *claim* to be very busy, and they probably won't believe it is always true. Moreover, if you really are so incredibly busy, how will you fit in the proposed work for them? Think about it. You need to convey the impression that you would like their business, but that it is not essential that you have it today. Desperation does not work. Confidence and calmness does.

Another side effect of always appearing to be frantically busy is that there is a distinct possibility that you will convey the impression that you are disorganized as well. This is a poor signal to be sending out. There is a good balance to be found in always making yourself available for potential business, but on your own terms and in your own time (within reason). Obviously you do not wish to come across as indifferent, but you should reserve the right to pace the flow of any new business advances to make sure that you deliver appropriately for your existing customers, because they pay the bills. When you are talking on the phone, make it clear that you are available to do the necessary work.

49 Try selling the opposite of everyone else

It may seem fashionable to promote yourself or your business as specialists. Somehow people think it is more reassuring if they have a 'specialism', and to be fair there is some evidence that certain specialists are able to charge more for their services. Yet experienced business people can usually fix a whole range of issues, so it is important for you to think broadly. This is very likely to increase your opportunities, your income and the breadth of your work. This in turn will introduce greater variety to your work.

Of course, this suggestion presupposes that you are indeed capable of doing more than one type of thing. In theory it is possible that you genuinely cannot, but most people have more than one talent, and those who are capable of working on their own are certainly at the more enterprising end of the spectrum, and are usually used to fixing a range of problems. Give it some thought. Try portraying yourself as a generalist, not a specialist. You could get more work, and you will in all probability enjoy yourself more by venturing into new areas that you haven't tried before.

50 Tell them it is simple (because you are experienced)

Tugging your beard and saying that something is really complicated does not inspire confidence and is as dismaying as a plumber staring at your boiler and declaring 'We'll never get the parts for this'. By all means appear thoughtful and reflective. Tell them that you have dealt with a similar issue before and that you know what to do – particularly if this is the first time you have spoken on the phone. A lot of work is commissioned not because the customers cannot do it themselves, but because they do not have the time. Consequently, it is often appropriate to tell them that they could certainly do the work themselves, but would it help if you took it off their 'Things to do' list for a certain price? At this point, speed and convenience may become more relevant than your precise skill set.

51 Offer to solve their issue quickly

Doing something quickly doesn't mean that the work is bad quality or bad value. It may be precisely what the customer wants. As the old story goes, if a portrait costs £10,000, the painter is charging that for a lifetime's experience, regardless of whether he or she does the job in a day or a month. The speed with which you can do something has absolutely no bearing on the value. An experienced mechanic might diagnose and cure a problem in half an hour. An amateur might take all day, and may even do a poorer job of fixing it. The fast solution may actually be the higher quality one, assuming that the person in question knows exactly what they are doing.

This approach is also a pleasant counterpoint to suppliers who want to make a job last longer so that they can charge more. A good maxim for those who work on their own is:

Don't string it out in order to charge a higher price.

Offer to fix something quickly based on the assumption that you are experienced enough to know what you are doing, and organized enough to schedule it in efficiently and get on with it. If it is a business issue that needs resolving, offer to do it as a commando raid in a reasonably short space of time (you will be able to judge the appropriate timing based on your intimate knowledge of your sector). If you do the job well, you will have a satisfied client, and you will have been paid a good price for a sensible outlay of time. In short, neither party will have wasted any time.

52 Be ready with examples of customers for whom you work

People love case histories, and when you catch them on the phone they don't usually have much time. They want easy anchor points on which to base their purchasing decision, just like references on a CV. They want to ask:

• Who else have you worked for?
• What did you do for them?
• Can I have some examples?

You need to anticipate these requests and, after a short while, you should be able to rattle these off effortlessly, even in your early days when you may actually be using examples from your previous corporate life. You do not always have to refer to something directly related to the task in hand, but you should become skilled at drawing on examples and making links between issues.

Customers do not always want people with direct experience of their field. Of course the narrow-minded ones might, but you wouldn't want them as customers anyway, now would you? Very often people in particular businesses have become too close to the issues that they encounter every day. This is sometimes called 'going native'. If they are smart enough to realize this, they will welcome a fresh perspective. That's where you come in. It is extremely likely that your skills are transferable and that they could benefit another business area if applied thoughtfully. So don't be sheepish about your skills – simply think broadly and suggest how your strengths could benefit the issue being discussed.

53 Don't start discounting before you have even met

Don't start discounting on the phone. Remember your central maxim from Chapter 3: 'Charge a premium price and do a great job' (p.40). State your rates clearly and without embarrassment. If they balk at the cost, say that you can discuss it when you meet and when you have better understood the nature of the possible work. Anyone who works on their own has examples of potential clients who have exclaimed 'How much?!', only to come back later with their tail between their legs having had a poor experience elsewhere with a cheaper alternative.

There are really only three variables at stake when a customer is considering whether to make a purchase: quality, price, and timing. Put simply, the three questions are:

• Will it do the job?
• How much will it cost?
• When can I have it?

When you are negotiating, it is essential to remember that you can always have some flexibility on any two of the three variables, but never on all three. For example, you may be able to reduce the price if you are given a longer time. You may be able to do it quicker if you can charge more. And no one will ever admit to wanting low quality, but things can be short-circuited.

A good way to remember this negotiating stance is to try starting every sentence with the word 'if'. This ensures that you interrelate all the variables so that you never give all three away and end up in a pickle. For example, 'If I have to deliver it by Friday, the price will have to increase'; 'If you need the price to reduce, I will need longer to do the job'.

The 'if' triangle

54 Have a system for noting your calls

Keep a full list of all your contacts and have a system for
contacting them – use the contact list and new business hit list
that we looked at in Chapter 2. Keep them right up to date.
Choose an appropriate contact frequency for your business that
does not represent pestering. By all means note some detail
about what was said if you think you might forget, but don't
clutter the list with irrelevant stuff that might impede your next
call. Staying organized in this area says volumes about your
reliability and efficiency.

- The appropriate timing of your call says that you are diligent
  but not desperate or aggressive
- The fact that you know when you last spoke shows that you
  are on the ball
- The fact that you did call back when you said you would
  means that you are thoroughly organized and are therefore
  likely to be similarly efficient when doing a job for the client
- If you have a new idea or have noted a development in their
  business circumstances to which you can refer, even better.

55 Be natural and human

One final point when you are looking for new business, and particularly if you are talking with someone for the first time on the phone. Be natural and remain true to your character. Keep your pride. Don't apologize for calling, and don't talk down what you have to offer. There is every chance that they will find your call helpful and interesting, and you'll never know unless you ask.

Remember one of the critical principles of running your own business: 'Only do business with people you like'. If they don't want to use you, it doesn't really matter. If they won't talk to you, it doesn't matter. Not everybody works with everyone else, and you will derive far more job satisfaction from working with people whose company you enjoy and who genuinely appreciate your contribution. In fact, many people leave larger companies precisely because they cannot find these qualities in their work. Therefore, there's not much point in working on your own if you simply end up replicating all the aspects of your previous working life that you were trying to change.

All you need is enough work to keep you stimulated and solvent. No adverse response is personal – it's just business. If it's not happening with a particular prospect, let it go, and keep your self-esteem intact. On the other hand, you will be jubilant when you have completed a successful call that has given you work. Then you will definitely know that you have tamed the telephone.

The ten golden rules of unsolicited calling*

1 Type out a list of people to call.
2 Print it out. If it's on the screen you won't do it.
3 Always print the phone number by the name. If you don't, you won't make the call.
4 Use a red pen to tick off your calls.
5 Never leave a message. If you do, you immediately cede control of the contact to the other person. This means that, the moment you call again, you are pestering.
6 If they are not there but someone else answers, ask for a good time to catch them, make a note, and call back. Do not be tempted to leave your name.
7 If you get voicemail, write down their mobile number and call them, or note any other information on the message and use it if appropriate.
8 When you do get through, make it sound as though it's the first time you've tried, even if it has taken weeks.
9 Make sure you can sell what you do in one sentence. Become adept at describing what you do rapidly and succinctly.
10 Always be cheerful and positive.

*Notice I have chosen not to call it 'cold-calling'. It is your job to make it warm, and the client may well welcome your call, so think positive.

Success Story: Steve Hunt, Mechanic

All mechanics are pretty much the same, you might think. But not in Steve's case. The guy was a demon on the telephone. He was very good at describing what he did in a charming, pithy way. His style rapidly forged relationships with dealers and parts suppliers who would favour his requests over those of his competitors.

And then he took his mastery of the telephone a step further by using it to expand his client base. He didn't subscribe to the received wisdom that people only call a mechanic as a distress purchase. He scoured the local directories and rang local businesses that he expected to own cars, vans and lorries. He offered them bulk discounts for regular servicing. He delivered door drops to the expensive houses in the area and followed up with a phone call to add some personal character to his marketing materials. He offered to come to them for emergencies. The majority had never come across such an outgoing mechanic.

He didn't use jargon when describing what needed doing. He worked hard to make himself available and he always delivered when he said he would. He fixed things quickly and so was able to command a premium price. He took business cards with him wherever he went and his satisfied customers started to augment his marketing efforts with their personal recommendations.

Steve was a success, and it all took off when he capitalized on his telephone skills. It was a good call.

Chapter 5 Taming the telephone

Checklist: what have you done?   ✓

1 Not called it 'cold-calling'   ☐

2 Admitted that the phone will never ring unless you market yourself   ☐

3 Understood that 100 calls will get 40 meetings and three jobs   ☐

4 Prepared your selling angles   ☐

5 Not used jargon to disguise what you do   ☐

6 Told them you are available   ☐

7 Tried selling the opposite of everyone else   ☐

8 Told them it is simple (because you are experienced)   ☐

9 Offered to solve their issue quickly   ☐

10 Been ready with examples of customers for whom you work   ☐

11 Not started discounting before you have even met   ☐

12 Had a system for noting your calls   ☐

13 Been natural and human   ☐

06
understanding time

In this chapter you will learn
- how everyone views time differently
- the two golden rules of time
- the six-month time lag
- how corporate time moves slower than normal time
- the Priority Matrix

Now we are going to look at the concept of time. If it sounds like a heavy subject, don't worry. We won't be investigating the speed of light or debating the pros and cons of the space–time continuum. Although, so many of us rush around that it's not a bad thing to pause and reflect for a moment or two. Have you ever asked yourself what time is for? Time passes whether we like it or not. How we measure the passage of time is one thing. How we describe it in universally acknowledged ways in order to be reasonably organized is another. Presumably that's why someone invented the calendar – in order for us all to know roughly where we are, or at least where we are supposed to be, at any given point. Perhaps one of the best definitions is that time was invented by humans to stop everything happening at once.

However, we need to answer this simple question:

What has time got to do with business?

The answer, as you might expect, is: absolutely everything. We have already established that there are really only three things that matter when you are delivering something for a customer, which are:

- Will it do the job?
- How much will it cost?
- When can I have it?

There it is loud and clear in the third point: how quickly can you meet the client's request? If you fail to understand how time affects your business, then the basis of most of your plans and all your personal expectations are likely to be wrong. This is vital to what you do all day because, although plenty of things will happen *eventually*, they may all come far too late for you to pay the bills. Sounds over-dramatic? Let's investigate.

56 Everyone views time differently

There are many dimensions to this assertion. Some of them make good sense. Others are a little more abstract. Yet they all have a direct effect on your ability to run a successful going concern, so let's consider a few of them.

First, as the person running the business, you will want to see progress and presumably some return on your effort and investment reasonably quickly, even if you are a very patient person. This desire has nothing to do with your customers whatsoever, and you need to be very careful that your agenda doesn't get in the way of your running a good operation or providing a decent service.

Think more about this. No single customer has the overview on your business that you do. You know the whole picture. You have a highly-tuned knowledge of how much work you have, what the cash flow is, whether you can cope with the work load or not, and a million other details. Anyone else you speak to has no idea of any of this. Therefore, you need to judge very carefully whether the speed with which you want to progress something is suitable for your customer. If it is not, then they will at worst sense your desperation or at best think you are hasty or strangely frantic.

Second, there are often customers who do actually *want* things done in a hurry. This may or may not be appropriate to the nature of your business or your circumstances at any given time. If what you provide takes time and consideration to produce, then you need to reconcile such impatient requests with your personal and business standards. Review your timing needs in relation to the possible outcomes that may occur if you hurry a job through. Here are some examples:

- In your rush to please someone at short notice, are you compromising on quality in a way that will come back to sully your reputation later?
- If you deliver at breakneck speed once, will they assume next time that this is the norm and ask for every job to be completed on that sort of timetable?
- By accepting a rush job, will you be displacing or inconveniencing an existing customer who always gives you sensible deadlines?

You need to consider these types of questions carefully and make sure that you do not create a noose for your own neck by establishing precedents that will be unhelpful later.

Third, bear in mind that, in many instances, something that takes longer to do or produce has a much higher perceived value. If a customer thinks that you have 'knocked something up quickly', then why should they wish to pay a higher price for it? Without being cynical, there are plenty of businesses in which it is preferable to take a little longer over something intentionally in order to emphasize the expertise that went into it. This observation is not intended to endorse the hoodwinking of customers by lying about how long something takes to do. It is however true that we live in an on-demand world, and the spirit of 'I want it now' can ruin your business if you give in too often. Make sure that, whenever humanly possible, you only accept appropriate deadlines for what you are being asked to do.

When you run your own business, there are two golden rules that are essential to your understanding of how time can affect your business:

The two golden rules of time

1 Everything you do will involve a six-month time lag
2 Corporate time moves slower than normal time.

Let's examine what these assertions mean.

57 Everything you do will involve a six-month time lag

Six months is an indicative round figure designed to illustrate a point. Of course it might not be six months in your line of work. It doesn't really matter what the precise figure is. What does matter is that, when you have decided upon a plan, nothing ever happens as quickly as you expect (unless it is something that you did *not* plan, in which case it may happen very quickly and unexpectedly).

Here is a hypothetical chain of events that describes an average job in a service business, from the moment you begin the run-up to it, to the day on which you complete it, and get paid.

Getting through

If you call a prospective customer today, it will probably take **two weeks** to get through, assuming that the person you need to contact is unavailable at the precise moment that you happen to want them to be in. We discussed in Chapter 5 the many possible reasons for this, and consequently it is reasonable to assume that you will not initiate your idea on the very first day that you think of it.

Planning the meeting

When you do eventually get through on the phone, the prospective client is very unlikely to be able to meet with you immediately to discuss what you have in mind. Let's say that they might be able to see you in **three weeks**.

Actually meeting

Most meetings are moved at least once before they occur. The chances of this happening to you are high, although the number of postponements may be related to the nature of your business. Remember that, until you are officially engaged to work for someone, you remain peripheral to the action. You will only become essential when you have been signed up, at which point you will probably be hugely in demand. The average is three postponements before the meeting actually takes place. That's another **three weeks**.

Time for them to consider

After you have met, there will always be some sort of delay. Most customers need time to consider things. They have lots to do other than deal with what you have to offer. They probably have colleagues to talk to about you, and they may have competitors whose proposals they can compare with yours. After some deliberation, even if there genuinely is work to be had from that potential customer, it could easily take **six weeks** to come through.

Doing the work

Once commissioned, it may only take you a week to do the work, and of course this depends completely on what you do for a living. Nevertheless, regardless of your speed in delivering the goods, there will be customer comments, changes of mind and approval delays that will probably take another **three weeks**.

Sending the bill out

Let's be generous and say that you will be able to bill the job **one week** after you have finished it. This assumes that you have a sufficiently efficient system of sending out invoices every week, and that there is no uncertainty about invoicing immediately after a job is finished. (There are always touchy moments for those who work on their own when the bill has been sent but the customer doesn't accept that the job is finished because they feel there is still something left to tidy up.)

Getting paid

It will most likely take them a minimum of **six weeks** to pay. Payment times vary hugely. Some retail and product-based transactions are settled on the spot. Some service projects are paid for within ten days, but these are the exception. At the other end of the scale, some companies take over 100 days to pay up. Some even have a deliberate policy of refusing to do so for 90 days. That's three months, which to the person who works on their own can be an unmitigated disaster for cash flow.

Without going into a moral debate about how quickly people should be paid, you can now see that the combined effect of all these stages is likely to be around **24 weeks**.

That's **six months** or, to be absolutely clear about this, **half a year**.

How the six-month time lag works

Getting through to a prospective customer	**2 weeks**
Delay before you can meet	**3 weeks**
Rescheduling of meeting two or three times	**3 weeks**
Time for them to consider your proposal	**6 weeks**
Doing the job	**3 weeks**
Sending the bill out	**1 week**
Time taken for you to be paid	**6 weeks**
Total time	**24 weeks**
24 weeks = six months = half a year	

Dramatic overstatement or business reality? Unfortunately, it is reality. You need to accept this fact quickly if you are to be a success on your own. This type of sequence is true to the majority of jobs – if you initiate something today, it is likely that the cheque will hit your doormat in about half a year. Once you have acknowledged this, you can reschedule your business plan, work out a much more realistic cash flow, and understand better the cycle of effort that you need to put in to get the work you need, when you need it.

This common-sense approach to accounting projections will stand you in much better stead than plugging in a mathematical formula from some accounting software or a bank's small business service. Be brutally honest with yourself and plan for the worst so that you will not be caught out.

We have already discussed how those who work on their own often fail to develop new business opportunities because they are supposedly too busy servicing existing business. Yet this six-month time lag equation demonstrates how short-sighted that approach is. By the time you are experiencing a lull in your current work, it could take *half a year* to reap the benefit of any renewed business effort. Unless you have a phenomenal stockpile of cash, this could prove fatal to your business. Therefore, without jeopardizing the quality of what you are currently up to, it is essential that you devote some time every month to developing new business possibilities.

58 Corporate time moves slower than normal time

Has the author lost his bearings here? Surely we all work to internationally-recognized standards of what time is, and we have all adhered to them for centuries? Whilst not disputing the accuracy of Greenwich meantime for one second (if you'll excuse the pun), it really is true that one person's perception of the *passage* of time can be completely different to another's. Think about how many times you have heard people say the following phrases:

'I can't believe it's Friday already.'

'This week has just flown by.'

'I don't know where the month went.'

'I can't believe it's Christmas so soon.'

Some would probably argue that there is only a finite amount of time in the world, and that if busy people haven't got enough, idle people must have too much. Certainly, if you haven't got much to do, time drags. If you are busy, it rushes by. You really do need to take this into account when you are dealing with customers and prospects who are moving at a different pace to your personal desires. This is not the same point as the six-month time lag that we have just looked at.

Corporate time is different from personal time for many reasons. The main one is that working in an office involves doing all sorts of things that you would not ordinarily choose to do. Sitting in meetings is a particular culprit. Most meetings are attended by too many people who would probably rather be doing something else. In some extreme cases, people working for companies can spend as much as four days a week in meetings. This prevents them from doing the things that all the time spent in the meetings has already agreed they should do, and it makes them wonder where the week went.

It is also very much in the interests of someone working for a company to appear busy, regardless of whether they really are or not. In a company, the work expands to fit the time available to do it, in which case it is very rare for someone to claim that they have very little to do. Thus, corporate time really can be slower than normal time. This means that you need to re-calibrate your timing plans and expectations when working with larger companies.

59 One day of personal time equals two weeks of corporate time

For anyone who runs their own business, the *New Equation of Time* is:

> *One day of personal time equals two weeks of corporate time.*

This equation has been developed by the author over five years and several hundred jobs. Here are some guidelines based on this discovery in order to help you to understand how to deal with larger companies:

- You need to multiply every anticipated timing by a factor of ten working days in order to get a better flavour of how long it might really take.
- When they say that there will be a decision tomorrow, it means in a fortnight at the earliest.
- This phenomenon works the other way round – if you take a month off, it is the equivalent of a customer taking two working days off. No one will notice, let alone care. You should build this holiday into your business plan at the beginning of the year and adjust the income and anticipated work around it.

The moral of this discovery for those who run their own business is brutally simple:

Whatever you plan to do, start now.

60 Whatever you plan to do, start now

Prevarication is one of the greatest enemies of anyone who works on their own. Never put off something that needs doing, and never deny the truth. Take it on the chin and get it done. Have a look at Chapter 7 ('Do not distinguish between nice and nasty things to do', p.87). If you delay something, it will simply be there staring you in the face tomorrow. And the day after. And the day after that.

We can categorically state that the spirit of 'Maybe tomorrow' or 'Mañana mañana' has no place whatsoever in the lexicon of anyone who works on their own. If this is your natural tendency, either you should abandon your plans to run your own business now, or you will already have battled really hard and succeeded in overcoming it.

Adopt the 'Think Do' principle we established in Chapter 1. If you are not a particularly organized person, at the very least you need to take on some of the trappings of someone who is, otherwise you won't be very effective on your own. Draw yourself a Priority Matrix with two axes based on urgent/not urgent, and important/not important. Now fill in your jobs to do.

- If it is urgent and important, do it now
- If it is urgent but not important, delegate it if you can (obviously this may be difficult because you work on your own, but you never know), or do it quickly first to get it out of the way
- If it is important but not urgent, think about what you need to do and plan when you are going to do it
- If it is neither important nor urgent, then why on earth are you doing it?

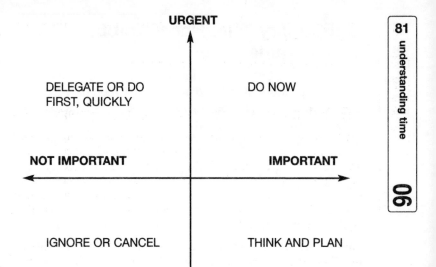

Priority matrix

Regardless of the method by which you manage to get organized, organization definitely needs to become one of your strengths. Keep reminding yourself that if it needs to be done, then it has to be done by *you*. The task won't go away, and it will usually get worse the longer you leave it. The passage of time will trip you up in the end, unless you stick to the golden rule:

Whatever you plan to do, start now.

Time is a big issue, but if you stick to the five principles covered in this chapter, then you will be that much closer to understanding how different people view it, and how understanding this can really help to increase your chances of being a success.

Cautionary Tale: Harry Knibb, Sales Trainer

Harry wasn't a particularly impatient guy, but he didn't give a moment's thought to the difference between how time is perceived by companies and individuals. He was selling sales training, and we all know that training is one of the first things to be cut in a budget if there are financial pressures. Harry always wanted things to follow his timing, and that isn't a desirable quality when you are running your own business.

One of the main consequences was that his expectations about the length of projects, and their gestation periods, was all wrong. So were his estimates as to when he would be paid for his work. So his first-year projections were about six months off the pace. What he failed to realize was that, when your income forecast is self-deluding, you always have the excuse to delay starting something on the grounds that the next project or payment is 'just around the corner'. So Harry ignored the maxim 'Whatever you want to do, start now.'

He also became an irritation to the companies that he worked for, because the frequency of his contact was usually out of step with their agenda. So, after making a series of overly keen calls and emails, he developed a reputation for being a bit desperate. Some clients concluded that he must be hard up. Others just didn't return his calls because he was becoming annoying.

Having failed to grasp the concept of time, Harry ended up with a lot of it on his hands.

Chapter 6 Understanding time

Checklist: what have you done? ✓

1 Acknowledged that everyone views time differently ☐

2 Realized that everything you do will involve a six-month time lag ☐

3 Admitted that corporate time moves slower than normal time ☐

4 Accepted that one day of personal time equals two weeks of corporate time ☐

5 Planned whatever you wanted to do, and started already ☐

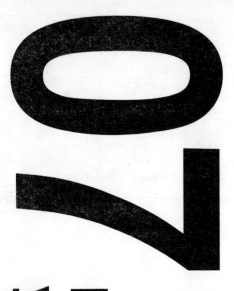

07

how to conduct yourself

In this chapter you will learn
- how to create a 'company culture' when you run your own business
- how to motivate yourself
- what to do and what not to do
- why you should only do business with people you like
- why talking to yourself is a good thing

We have covered many of the emotional and practical aspects of how to run your own business. There is another utterly essential element that books cannot really teach you, but which requires careful attention nonetheless. It is not tangible. You can't buy it. You can't quantify or measure it. You may be able to acquire a few of the skills that allow you to believe that you have got 'it' about right, although you will never know for sure. So what is this elusive quality? It is how to conduct yourself.

When you work for yourself, the way that you come across is absolutely paramount. Within minutes, seconds even, you can convey completely the wrong impression. Your manners, your dress, your attitude – they all count for a great deal. They can lose the interest or respect of your potential customer in an instant. When you launch your own business, you owe it to yourself to consider very carefully what sort of image you wish to convey.

61 You *are* the company culture

You need to confront the fact that, when you work on your own, you *are* the company culture. There are no hazy mission statements to fall back on, no Human Resources department, and no glossy brochure to cover up for shoddy behaviour. You need to behave as you would like others to behave. What does that mean? Well, disregarding personal style for a moment, there are some basic principles of good conduct to which you should adhere. For example:

- Be polite
- Be realistic
- Turn up on time
- Return calls when you say you will
- Pay your bills immediately
- Over-deliver if you wish, but never under-deliver.

You can create your own list of this type based on your personal preferences and the nature of your business. Over time, you will undoubtedly receive back as much good behaviour as you dish out. You will gain a reputation for high standards, integrity and honesty. Repeat business will follow.

Or, put another way, if you are small-minded, you will lose good customers and attract those who are also small-minded and unreliable. At an early stage, map out what you believe to be the important parts of how to conduct your business, and use that as a blueprint to determine how you should conduct *yourself*, and in turn what you expect and desire of others. This will stand you in good stead if you have to confront a dilemma about whether to decline some business, or if you have to take the harsh decision to inform an existing customer that you will no longer work with them. Making such a fundamental decision on the spot often comes across as impetuousness or impatience, but if you have thought through your principles carefully, you can state calmly and clearly that their way of doing things does not tally with yours. That's your right as someone who works on their own.

62 Only do business with people that you like

This is quite a tricky area but it really is worth spending the time to work out how you feel about your business relationships. Naturally, if you work in a service business or run a retail outlet you can't vet everybody with whom you have a transaction. But you *can* choose the nature of your suppliers and associates. And as you develop your own personal style, you will become better at working out what other people are like to deal with. Eventually, you should be in a position whereby it is you who chooses to do business with somebody, not the other way round.

Why is this important? Because ultimately if you do not enjoy the company of the people with whom you have to interact, you will effectively have engineered a state of affairs in which you don't like what you do. This is a disaster for anyone who runs their own business. Indeed, the whole point of working on your own is to design a set-up that suits your particular style. Of course, sometimes it takes a while for someone to show their true colours, and there will be times when somebody you really like lets you down. Unfortunately, there is nothing you can do about this, and it is undoubtedly true that any disappointments will be felt harder by you as an individual than by companies in the collective sense. However, in the long run, your judgement will improve with experience, and your goal should be only to do business with the people that you like.

63 Subsume your ego

There is a huge difference between having a particular personal style and having a big ego. Personal style is distinctive, desirable and an important element of why people choose to do business with you. Ego is destructive, selfish and impedes business relationships. If you want to be a success, and you have a big ego, you need to have a personal truth session and bury it. This is not so that you become an automaton with no character, but so that your skills and qualities can come to the fore and be seen to be of value by potential customers without your ego detracting from them. If you are showboating all the time, this is unlikely to be the case.

It often helps if you let your customers believe or claim that many of your ideas are theirs. You will get more repeat business. If you make someone look good, they will be eternally grateful. This is not sycophancy. When you hear that someone has 'bought into' one of your ideas, it means they have joined in and helped to convince themselves of the value of it. This is outstanding selling, and cannot happen if you keep banging on about how it was 'my idea'.

Another way of reconciling this with your ego is to remember that, once a client has paid you for your work, it is actually theirs. In the case of tangible products, this is obviously self-evident. But in the grey area of ideas and advice, even the 'copyright' of your recommendations becomes your clients' property, assuming that you have negotiated an appropriate price and taken intellectual property issues into account. It should in fact be a genuine piece of flattery if a client chooses to champion your work and go so far as to claim it as their own.

64 Do not distinguish between nice and nasty things to do

What a strange idea! It is human nature to say 'I love doing x' and 'I hate doing y'. Sadly, now that you are your own boss, you need to stop making the distinction between the two. Why? Because it was your decision to go it alone, and whatever needs doing has to be done and is ultimately entirely for your own personal benefit. Even if the task is working out how much tax to pay, it is worth doing well because if you don't, you will be the one to lose out.

It is also inaccurate to presuppose that something you expect to be nasty will actually turn out to be so. In reality, the outcome of a situation that you are anxious about is frequently the opposite of what you expect it to be. This may sound false but it is actually true. For instance, can you imagine how you might have a better meeting firing someone than giving them a pay rise? No? Have a look at these two examples.

Proof that nasty things can turn out to be nice

Employer: I'm very sorry but after a lot of discussion and anxiety I'm afraid we can't keep you in this job any longer.

Employee: I can't say I'm surprised. I haven't been coping very well and I haven't been happy. I was thinking of going travelling instead.

Proof that nice things can turn out to be nasty

Employer: I am pleased to tell you that we have agreed a £3,000 pay rise for you.

Employee: I'm really disappointed. I was expecting a minimum of £5,000.

So you see, that supposedly nasty cold-call looming on your checklist might well be the very thing that makes you most happy this month. Go on. Get to it!

65 Talk to yourself

Talking to yourself is not a sign of madness. It is actually an extremely helpful way for someone who works on their own to clarify things when no one else is around. Saying things out loud is a highly constructive thing to do. Go on, say it out loud now. You can eliminate all manner of nonsense from letters if you take the trouble to read them out loud. Frequently, they sound ludicrous when you read them back. You know the sort of thing: 'Please do not hesitate to contact myself ...' You would never speak like that, so don't write that way either.

Talking out loud also cures twaddle and jargon on presentation charts, waffle in marketing material, and spouting garbage on the telephone. If you practise your telephone pitch out loud and conclude that you sound like a twit, then that is clearly time well spent.

Another benefit of talking to yourself is that at least you are guaranteed a decent conversation and, although you may disagree with yourself, at least you won't have a flaming row! Despite what the amateur psychologists say, it's healthy, it's amusing, and for those of you poor people who miss the office, it provides a bit of banter about the place as well.

66 Remind yourself of all the positive things you have done

This is not a piece of self-delusion therapy. It is simply the knack of staying positive. All self-employed people suffer from some form of self-doubt. You don't have colleagues congratulating you on a job well done, so you need to generate your own humble form of self-congratulation. Think about it. No one else is going to bother, so you need to find a private way to celebrate your successes and keep your confidence levels up.

Consider these ideas for reminding yourself that you are actually pretty good at what you do and that you deserve a pat on the back:

- Write down your income
- Write down your profit
- Say out loud: 'I am still in business'
- Choose which recent business transaction was your favourite
- Ask a customer if they will write a reference for you
- Ask your partner or a friend if they think you are any good at what you do
- Invent an ingenious plan for the near future
- Calculate whether you can afford a holiday soon
- Book a holiday
- If you have rivals, consider whether they are doing as well as you

Remember this straightforward maxim:

Everything you achieve, you have done yourself.

67 Never moan

Moaning is one of the most unattractive features of any personality. Whose company would you prefer? Someone with a positive, optimistic outlook or someone who spends the whole time bellyaching about things that aren't going well? Moaning is unacceptable for anyone who works on their own. Why? Because it is actually an admission of failure. If you don't agree, here is a simple translation of a moaner's conversation to illustrate the point:

Bloke in pub: 'Business is really tough at the moment and things aren't going very well.'

There are two possible translations of this remark:

'I am not talented enough to get the work I want.'

or:

'I am too lazy to get the work I need.'

This is not an exaggeration. If you run your own business, then your fortunes are entirely in your hands. You can invoke as many higher powers as you like, blame macro-economic conditions, and invent reams of blether about precisely why you don't have enough work at the moment. None of this smokescreen will disguise the fact that you haven't had the wit or the determination to go and get it. This is not some assertion cooked up by a motivation guru or a sales zealot. It is cold, hard logic. So type it up and stick it on the wall: *No moaning*.

There is one other essential part of the 'No moaning' credo. Never be tempted to join in with a customer who is moaning. You can sympathize briefly, but then it is your job to suggest ways in which you can make it better, otherwise these dreadful people will rapidly turn you into a moaner too.

68 Never drink during the day

Does this point really need clarification? Then go back and work for a company. This is a no-brainer. The same goes for drugs and anything else that has the capacity to turn you into a blithering idiot during work hours. Save it for the weekend! If you ever receive a call from a customer in the afternoon and you are less than *compos mentis*, your reputation will be on the slide immediately. 'I wouldn't use him, he's a bit of a drinker' is not how you would wish to be described around town. If you really do have to have a near-compulsory jolly with a customer one day, then turn your mobile off and return any calls when you are sober, saying that unfortunately you were in an all-day meeting or out of town. Never get involved in important business when you are in danger of talking rubbish.

69 Never watch daytime TV

As with drinking, watching daytime TV is the rapid road to Loserville. What makes this so obvious?

- You should be working
- You won't learn anything
- After a short while, your IQ will probably fall.

If you disagree with this and insist on watching this drivel, then you only have two possible courses of action:

1 Reduce the quality of your work from now on to reflect your new low-level intellect
2 Lower your prices immediately to reflect your diminished aspirations.

70 Never finish a day before deciding what to do the next morning

This simple little discipline works incredibly well. It is outstandingly easy to do, and is the best ever way of ensuring a good night's sleep. Simply write down what you have to do the next day and, if appropriate, allocate the necessary time for it. Now you can relax. There are many subsidiary benefits to this approach. First, it is impossible to forget to do something because it is written down. Second, you come across as totally on the ball because you genuinely *do* know what you are doing the next day. And third, you don't have to worry about the tasks for the next day so you can go and have that drink after all.

71 Never do anything unless you know why you are doing it

How blindingly obvious is this statement? It would be a good principle for all businesspeople to abide by. Actually, it applies to anything you ever do in your whole life. This is so profoundly irrefutable that it is worth stating again:

Never do anything unless you know why you are doing it.

It stands to reason. Think carefully about what you are doing and why you are doing it. Your time is your potential money. If you are doing something unnecessary, then for every minute you do so, you are shooting yourself in the foot. Only do the things that matter. Your time is too precious to approach it any other way.

72 Have reserve plans for every day

When you start out working on your own, you may well quite naïvely assume that the shape of tomorrow will be exactly as it is written in your personal organizer. Nothing could be further from the truth! Just when you have put a suit on, on a day when you think you have three meetings, they may have all been cancelled by 9.30 a.m. If that does happen, it is not acceptable to sit around and do nothing on the grounds that everything has changed. In fact, you should assume every day that everything *will* change.

Being incapable of adapting rapidly is a big warning sign for anyone who works on their own. Expressing dismay that everything has changed at short notice conveys the impression that it is easy to catch you on the hop and that you are a bit of a plodder. Life's a mess – roll with it and enjoy the ride!

You need Plans B, C and so on that you can engage immediately when all the other activities fall away. The trick to avoid disappointment is to work out that this *will* happen *before* it happens. Then when it does, which it undoubtedly will, instead of being aghast at this extraordinary development and going into a flat spin, you simply reach for your Plan B file. Let's have a look at what a Plan B might be, and relish in the thought that the wonderful thing about Plan B is that Plan B is often more productive than Plan A.

73 Remember that Plan B is often more productive than Plan A

Here are 12 examples of things that anyone can do to generate a Plan B.

1 As a matter of course, you should read all the trade press related to your business, and that which your potential customers read, plus anything else that stimulates you. Collect ideas and articles, and use them to generate initiatives and give you the basis for a speculative phone call or proposal.

2 If an ex-customer or colleague surfaces somewhere in a new job, call them immediately, and keep an eye out for information on the new market that they have entered. This is how you will extend your customer base beyond its current shape.

3 Have good data sources, become familiar with them, and use them to generate ideas. In particular, remember that trends change all the time, so you cannot claim to be on top of developments if you don't check them regularly.

4 Read more books than your customers. Barely anyone in any industry has ever read what they are supposed to. If you have, you can help by introducing new ideas and by being the authority on a specific subject.

5 Collect interesting quotes that may help to liven up presentations or marketing materials. It is a tricky business looking for inspiration at the precise moment that you need it. The whole thing is much easier if you make a habit of collecting stimulating quotes all the time. Then when you need some inspiration, you can simply reach for your quotes file.

6 Look up a word in the dictionary every day to make yourself more erudite (look that one up if you need to). Obviously this is a matter of personal choice, but we only use a fraction of the words available in our language and it can become very dull. The beauty of working for yourself is that, if you want to look up a word on the spot, then you usually can. People in companies rarely want to admit to a colleague that they don't know the meaning of a word, let alone that they don't possess a dictionary. Here's a fun little exercise to increase your word power. Look up these words and see if

Abrogate	vb	to cancel an agreement
Baronial	adj	acting like a powerful businessman
Chimera	n	an unrealistic dream or idea
Diatribe	n	a bitter critical attack
Egregious	adj	shockingly bad
Fresco	n	wall painting using watercolours on wet plaster
Garrulous	adj	constantly chattering or talkative
Hubris	n	pride or arrogance
Interpolate	vb	to insert into a conversation or text
Jocund	adj	cheerful or merry
Kaput	adj	ruined or broken
Languorous	adj	in a vague, dreamy state
Mollify	vb	to make someone less angry
Necromancy	n	sorcery or communication with the dead
Omnipotent	n	all powerful
Peripatetic	adj	travelling from place to place
Quasi-		almost but not really
Riparian	adj	on the bank of a river
Snig	vb	to drag a felled log by a cable
Tremulous	adj	trembling from fear or excitement
Utilitarian	adj	useful rather than beautiful
Vapid	adj	dull and uninteresting
Waspish	adj	bad tempered or spiteful
Xerox	n	photocopy
Yorker	n	cricket ball bowled just under the bat
Zephyr	n	a soft gentle breeze

vb = verb; adj = adjective; n = noun

your dictionary definitions tally with those given in the list. At least it will force you to buy a dictionary and open it.

Few things are more pointless than an unopened dictionary.

7 Improve your grammar and phraseology so that you can express yourself better than your customers and competitors, obviously without turning into a pompous, condescending fool. In certain businesses, you can even sell this as a skill in its own right because all companies can improve how they communicate. The overall effect will be to reinforce the fact that you are good at what you do and can express yourself well.

8 Hobbies and projects are good to have at hand, so long as they do not take over your working life. They can provide an excellent counterbalance to work if you have a lot of intensive stuff to do over a sustained period, and customers will find your other talents interesting because they complement their perception that you are an enterprising person with plenty of ideas and energy.

9 More specifically, when you have achieved something extra-curricular, make it part of your CV and sales patter. People are interested, and it adds a human dimension to the person behind the business skills that they are being offered.

10 Constantly rewrite your CV, redefining your skills again and again to reflect what you are best at, and what you enjoy doing most, based on the new work you are doing. Don't forget that what you are best at and what you enjoy most are often strongly related. This is very much part of the joy of working on your own – you can dictate, within reason, the nature of the work that you choose to do, and mould it as you develop your understanding of yourself.

11 Regularly examine the shape of your business so that you can rattle off the facts to your clients. For example:

- How many clients did you have in year 1/2/3?
- How many jobs did you do in year 1/2/3?
- How much repeat business did you have in year 2?

12 Look at the bottom of your contact list and call everyone below the Pester Line

If after all those suggestions you are still able to claim that you have no idea what to do with your time, you should definitely not be running your own business. And whether you agree with the ideas on how you should behave or not, you should definitely now be able to draw up your own rules of engagement, so that you are never unsure about how to conduct yourself. Once you do, you will have created your own 'company culture', and your potential customers will be left in no doubt as to what you stand for.

It is then up to your potential clients to decide whether your style suits them, and if you have conducted yourself well, then it is very likely that it will.

Success Story: Kate Taylor, Hospitality Consultant

Kate was a presentable lady who advised hotels, restaurants and clubs on how they could improve their handling of hospitality. She was a troubleshooter who could usually improve things herself, but was broad-minded enough to know her limitations and involve others where the task warranted it.

Her clients ended up loving her above all because of her attitude. She always gave spontaneous responses on the phone, she always returned calls rapidly, she turned up on time, and she was always positive. One way or another, clients always reckoned that Kate could fix it, and she usually could.

So what made her so different? Kate realized that she was the company culture. She behaved precisely as she would like others to be with her. She was very organized; she never moaned to her clients; she never criticized her competitors, in fact, sometimes she even recommended them if she had a lot on. And yet she remained true to her character and upheld her own standards, so she felt fulfilled.

In short, she was exactly the sort of person that we would all love to do business with, so she got plenty.

Chapter 7 How to conduct yourself

Checklist: what have you done? ✓

1 Acknowledged that you *are* the company culture ☐

2 Only done business with people you like ☐

3 Subsumed your ego ☐

4 Not distinguished between nice and nasty things to do ☐

5 Talked to yourself ☐

6 Reminded yourself of all the positive things you have done ☐

7 Never moaned ☐

8 Never drank during the day ☐

9 Never watched daytime TV ☐

10 Never finished a day before deciding what to do the next morning ☐

11 Never done anything unless you knew why you were doing it ☐

12 Had reserve plans for every day ☐

13 Remembered that Plan B is often more productive than Plan A ☐

08

meetings can be fun

In this chapter you will learn
- what to do when you secure a meeting
- what to do in meetings
- what to do after meetings
- how to ask what is on a client's mind and offer to fix it
- how to be more positive than everyone else all the time

Meetings. The very word invokes feelings of dread in some people. Even people who appear to be very confident in any other situation can freeze up and behave strangely. Yet with the right approach, meetings do not have to be daunting at all. Actually, they can be great fun, so let's have a look at some of the techniques that can make this a possibility.

74 When you secure a meeting, get organized straightaway

Efficiency is a sophisticated form of laziness.

Give this claim some careful thought. The more sorted you are, the less you need to panic. The better organized you are, the less time you will waste faffing about at the last minute in a state of disarray, and the more time you will have to enjoy yourself on your own terms. There is also a strong chance that the quality of what you produce will be higher, better considered and more fulfilling.

As soon as you have secured a meeting, take the time to work out exactly what you need in order to make it a success. This might include:

• Your CV
• Client list
• Case histories
• Examples of what you produce
• A list of ways in which you may be able to help (see p.102)
• A proposal or the outline of one
• Research or observations on their market and the issues they face
• Price list
• Terms of business.

If the need for these materials is fairly obvious, then immediately print them off and assemble them in a sensible way, with enough copies for everyone. How many times have you been to a meeting where people that have never been mentioned before turn up? You need to anticipate this and have spares of everything that matters so that you come across as professional and can address your ideas to the attendees who are going to have a direct bearing on the purchasing decision.

Now put your materials in a folder marked with the name of the people you are meeting and, if you need to, the date (but bear in mind that it will almost certainly change). If it needs more thought than that, either do the thinking now or write the preparation time in your personal organizer straightaway, always leaving plenty of time to do it before the day. This is particularly important because, if it does need more thought, it is highly likely that you will uncover more complicated issues when you do get round to reviewing it. If this is the case, then preparing moments before the meeting will be cutting it too fine.

We talked in Chapter 6 about the 'Think Do' principle that will serve you well when running your own business. Apply this to your meeting preparation and to what you do after you have had the meeting and have agreed that there are things to be done. There is often quite a gap between a meeting being arranged and it actually taking place. This can cause problems because, if you don't get organized now, you may well forget the subtleties of what the meeting is truly about, or indeed, what you have *chosen* to make it about. This may sound odd, but many people just write 'meeting with x' in the diary and think no more about it until the day before. This is hopeless. The clever angles are usually all lurking in the original phone call, and the only way to capture these is to *do it now.*

The same is true after a meeting. All the details and nuances are fresh in your mind and, although some issues may certainly require longer consideration, the chances are that your first instincts about roughly what needs to be done in response to a particular issue are about right. Make those decisions now and prepare your response. Under no circumstances convince yourself that it's okay to ignore it all because the follow-up meeting or your official response isn't due for a couple of weeks. By then you will have forgotten some of the finer points, and your response will be poorer as a result. With this organized approach, you can never be caught out by a meeting, even in the very unlikely event that you have forgotten all about it until the last minute.

Another important activity related to this level of organizational discipline is to examine your personal organizer often, not only to survey that day's appointments, but to look ahead and anticipate your flow of work. Thinking ahead is your best ally in the tricky business of dealing with many things at once. The better you are at doing things now, the more freedom you will have to accept other speculative work as and when it crops up.

It also reduces your worry levels because you know for sure that you really *are* prepared for something, no matter how far in the future it is, and now you can relax and get on with something else, be it work or pleasure.

75 Get chronological

Put your files in the order in which the meetings are due so that, on any given morning, you can simply reach for the relevant folder and walk out of the door. As the meeting dates change, change the chronological order of your prepared files. This approach completely circumnavigates the sort of panic that usually precedes a meeting for which you have not prepared. Remember, now that you work on your own, it is *your* choice whether you wish to be prepared or not. You no longer have the excuse of blaming someone else or other external (and supposedly uncontrollable) factors – although as we have already established, these are not usually valid excuses anyway. Nor do you have so many other distractions, unless you deliberately choose to allow something else to get in your way.

There are, of course, those who claim that the last minute, student-style 'essay crisis' approach to preparation also works for them in business. This really doesn't make any sense at all and usually comes across as a pretty thin argument. Whilst it may be true that certain characters only pull their finger out and do the necessary work when they are under pressure and so forced to, this is a dreadful way to operate when you work for yourself. It gives you no time for reflection or improvement of your proposals; only one attempt at a given issue; and usually mistakes creep in, making you look unprofessional. It is far better to contemplate something in good time and be completely ready for the task at hand.

76 Research everything thoroughly

Being well prepared wins you business and gains you customers. Do plenty of research so that you know what you are talking about and have some interesting lines of enquiry to pursue. Try some of the following:

• Investigate the company on the internet and via any other sources you can obtain

- Critique these sources so that you have an opinion on how the company presents itself
- Be inquisitive. Ask *why?* several times in a row to work out why things are as they are
- Write down a list of issues that affect the potential customer
- Find out as much as you can about the customer as an individual
- Are there colleagues involved too?
- What are their issues and angles?
- Go to the meeting with lots of informed observations
- Take a list of questions to stimulate conversation
- Draw up a list of some ways in which you can help.

77 Give the client a list of ways in which you can help

Draw up a list of ways in which you think you can help the prospective client. This list is an absolute winner. No one can resist reading it for a start. The fact that you have made plenty of suggestions proves that you have plenty of ideas, and that you have been thinking about their business, which is always flattering because people always love talking about their own area. This level of enterprise and enthusiasm also means that it doesn't matter if you have made a couple of inaccurate assumptions, because they will be seen as forgivable in relation to your obvious keenness for the other matters in hand.

During the thousand or more meetings in which this approach has been tested, on average a minimum of two things on your list will be appropriate to the potential customer that day. Rest assured, that's two more than most speculative suppliers come up with. It is also a thoughtful and diligent thing to do because the ideas are specific to their business, and have the power to elevate you above the normal supplier who only brings along the standard materials that they clearly use for every other meeting.

What will set you apart is the degree to which you are inquisitive. Many people go into meetings simply trying to find a home for products or services that they already have, and then selling them as hard as possible. This approach has only limited success because it depends entirely on whether there is potential in the market for that sort of thing *at that precise moment*. With your more inquisitive approach, you will be suggesting ideas and asking questions. The opportunity lies in listening carefully to the answers, and adapting your skills to see if you can help at all. Chances are that you will be able to.

78 Include things that you *could* do, even if you have never done them

It is fine to stick to known territory when you are launching your business, but after a while you may find your work a little monotonous and so wish to broaden your scope. Alternatively, you may have reached the stage where the demand and income for your core offerings do not have enough value to sustain the income or margin that you desire. This broader approach of suggesting what you *could* do (rather than what you have always done before) could lead you into some very interesting areas and might serve you well.

It is certainly worth trying if you find that your standard list of suggestions is not generating enough work. This may mean that the way in which you are describing what you offer is not striking the right sort of chord, or that there is not enough of a market for it at the moment. If so, you could reinvigorate your business by broadening your offering.

Later on in your solo life, if you have become somewhat bored with the sameness of your work, the value of offering to do things you have never done before will be stimulating and re-energizing. If you do receive a favourable response to a proposal, you will enjoy the challenge of working out how to do it, and will probably learn new skills in the process. Don't be scared of this – you will never find yourself proposing something that is so far beyond your skill set that you genuinely could not cope with the new challenge of doing it.

79 Ask what is on the client's mind at the moment and offer to fix it

Ask what is currently on the potential customer's checklist. Everyone has a checklist, and the average contains about 20 to 25 items. There is an approximate mathematical reason for this. If someone has very little to do (say, five things or less), there is little point in having a list because they can remember the items easily enough. On the other hand, if someone has so much to do that the number of tasks exceeds, say, 30, then they won't write down any more than that because the list will be too daunting. Human nature dictates that no one wants to stare at a seemingly endless list of things to do because it will be too depressing. So, even if there genuinely *are* more things to do than that, they certainly won't bother to write them down.

Therefore, the average list will have 20 or so things on it. This makes the author feel sufficiently busy and yet just about in control of what they are doing. The top three problems on it will probably be fixable by the owner of the list or by one of their colleagues. Anything that is below item number ten on their list of things to do, and is still there at the end of every week, is the sort of thing that you should offer to fix. Everyone has them. After a while they can't even remember why the item was put on the list in the first place. Often they have been asked by a boss to do it and they can barely remember why. You can even ask them what they would regard as a fair price to remove it from the list, and decide if that represents a viable amount for your purposes. Few can resist the offer of having a troublesome item like this removed from their list, and don't forget that you can often negotiate the price after you have established the need.

80 Listen more than you talk

This shouldn't really need any explanation. The old adage goes that you have two ears and one mouth, and should use them in that proportion. Listening hard unlocks all manner of issues that will enable you to help with, comment on, rectify, debate and, above all, engage your potential customer. If possible, you should ask a simple question that requires only one answer. Then shut up and pay attention. An example of such a question might be:

'What is bothering you most at the moment?'

Multiple questions don't work very well because it is rare that all the points are actually answered in the one response. An example of a bad question might be:

'Why is that an issue – I thought David had dealt with that last month and wasn't it supposed to be part of Project Pineapple anyway?'

This gives the potential client every opportunity to choose not to answer the question or, even if they genuinely did intend to answer it, to become distracted by one of the subsidiary points and so not really get to the main one. This serves no purpose and is to your detriment because it significantly reduces the chance of you finding out anything useful. It is far better to ask about one thing, hear the reply, understand it, and then move on to the next one.

81 Be more positive than everyone else in every meeting

People enjoy having meetings with positive, interesting people. This is not only true of business, but of any social encounter. The corollary of this is that no one enjoys meeting with a negative person. Consequently, it is essential that you can never be accused of being such a person.

Unfortunately, a lot of people have to do business with boring people who don't say what they mean and don't contribute anything positive. This needn't necessarily matter (provided you can retain your sense of humour in any given meeting) because by comparison you can only come across as more positive and alert than they are. Many people in business are simply 'killers' – those who constantly block ideas but never actually suggest any themselves. They bring everything down and even have the capacity to make *you* look bad by association if you do not have your wits about you. Do not let this happen. It is your job to remain enthusiastic (see Chapter 9, 'Staying sane and relentlessly enthusiastic'), because this will ensure that you are always a pleasure to have at meetings and are a constant source of helpful suggestions.

Now that you run your own business, you need never behave in a negative way. Go into meetings like a breath of fresh air, brimming with ideas. Enthusiasm is infectious. Many issues are tricky, but that doesn't mean that they have to be dealt with in a dull or negative way. Tackle the tough stuff head on, and come up with lots of ways of improving things. Customers love it, if only because it is often such a contrast to those who are happy to potter along and have a good old moan without suggesting anything positive. And of course the best compliment you can receive is when your customers always look forward to having meetings with you because of the difference you make in every encounter.

82 Never be late

Being late is just plain rude. In most cases, it is also totally avoidable and completely inexcusable. It doesn't take a genius to realize that if you have never been to the venue of a meeting before, you should allow extra time so that you have some leeway for heading to the wrong end of a very long street or underestimating the length of a journey. If you do turn up early, you can use the time to relax and run through what you plan to say once more. There's nothing wrong with saying that you had an idea on the way to the meeting. In fact, it proves that you are constantly thinking about the client's business issues.

A happy side effect of this approach is that, if it is *they* who are late, you will begin the meeting with something of a psychological upper hand. Stay calm and take it all in your stride. By comparison you will seem professional and prepared, which will imply that if they do end up engaging your services, you will be likely to deal with their work in the same orderly way.

Put another way, no one wants to do business with a breathless, shambolic person. This is an important point which is closely linked to the accuracy of your self-perception. You will have had occasions where you have been dismayed by someone else's business conduct, and we examined in Chapter 7 how you can work out how *you* should behave. Meeting etiquette is merely an extension of this philosophy, and you would never want to feel that you come across as poorly as any of those people in the past whom you feel have been a let down. So turn up on time.

83 Be spontaneous and act naturally

If you are asked for a proposal, an opinion or a price, suggest one straightaway. This does not convey a hurried approach. Nor does it suggest that you make things up on the hoof. It only confirms your experience in dealing with things quickly and authoritatively.

Remember that you no longer have to consult with a colleague because you haven't got any. Sometimes it is actually worth pointing this fact out to the potential customer. A lot of people fall into the trap of saying 'I'll have a think about that and get back to you'. Of course, if the problem is highly complex, you may want to retire gracefully to consider it further. But most of the time, in doing so you are simply introducing another barrier to the sales process, and creating another delay which is quite unnecessary. Go on instinct!

Your general attitude should be:

- You have done this many times before and you can comment immediately
- You know precisely what you are all about, so you can have an opinion on the spot
- You know your pricing structures intimately and you can quote the job now
- You are completely on top of your availability and you can talk about timings now
- Overall, you completely understand what they are talking about, and your approach tallies well with their needs.

These are the sorts of qualities that you should be conveying in all your meetings. They will ensure that, more often than not, your meetings are indeed fun. They are also the qualities of a successful person who knows their subject well and has a confident demeanour.

And that person is you.

Cautionary Tale: Roger Random, Freelance Graphic Designer

You all know the kind of guy – a bit scruffy, a bit vague on the phone, and rather disorganized. That was Roger, freelance graphic designer. He certainly managed to secure some meetings and get some work, but it was mainly through personal recommendation, so a fair amount of the 'pre-selling' had already been done.

He rarely thought much about a meeting before it happened. Of course he was ready with the design work if he had been commissioned. But when it came to new business meetings, he didn't research the clients beforehand, and he had no particular system for presenting his own capabilities. Couple that with a fairly wayward dress sense, and the first impression he created was one of relative apathy.

This approach was not a success. Everyone expects designers to be a bit trendy, and they allow for that. But prospective customers do not expect them to look unkempt, or to lack initiative. Many people actually take it as a signal that their business is unimportant. If they are in any doubt in this area, then it only takes one stray remark or someone turning up late to lose the job.

Which is what happened more often than not with Roger. He should have been on time and offered lots of ways in which he could help. But he didn't relish meetings, and nor did his prospective clients after they ended up seeing him. Which was a shame, because he was actually quite a nice bloke.

It wasn't Roger's grand design to return to salaried work in an agency, but that's what happened.

Chapter 8 Meetings can be fun

Checklist: what have you done?   ✓

1 Secured a meeting, and got organized
   straightaway ☐

2 Got chronological ☐

3 Researched everything thoroughly ☐

4 Given the client a list of ways in which you
   can help ☐

5 Included things that you *could* do, even if
   you have never done them ☐

6 Asked what is on the client's mind at the
   moment and offered to fix it ☐

7 Listened more than you have talked ☐

8 Been more positive than everyone else in
   every meeting ☐

9 Never been late ☐

10 Been spontaneous and acted naturally ☐

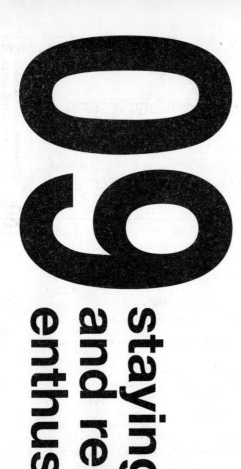

09
staying sane
and relentlessly
enthusiastic

In this chapter you will learn
- how to take the issues seriously, but not yourself
- why you should not do the same thing for too long
- the importance of time off and how to build it into your year plan
- why hobbies are a great idea
- how to get your working environment right

Stay sane and relentlessly enthusiastic? Has the author lost the plot? Surely it can't be possible? Oh yes it can, and here's how.

84 Take the issues seriously, but not yourself

This is a maxim that really, really works. Customers want their issues taken seriously, but this doesn't mean that you have to do things in a boring way. Earnest subject matter does not mean that the people dealing with it have to be in a permanent state of melancholy. So relax and don't take it all so seriously.

Humour and lightness of touch are great ways of staying calm and sane. A good laugh can really take the pressure off. On the other hand, being downhearted too frequently makes you annoyed with yourself, and you can be sure that it's no barrel of laughs for those around you either. This is not to suggest that you wear a revolving bow tie and clown suit to your next meeting. But try some of these ideas for lightening up your day:

- Take some interesting photos of a hobby or holiday to your next meeting
- Take a customer a small present such as a box of chocolates
- Send them an amusing article or quote from the paper
- Video a programme that you think they might like that has absolutely nothing to do with work.

You get the idea. These are pleasant and interesting things to do. They are not strictly work, but they will make work more enjoyable for you and your customers.

85 Never do one thing for too long

It is a rare person who enjoys doing the same thing over and over again for a very long time. That could mean several hours on the same day. It could mean most days of the week for three months, or most weeks of the year for five years. The ratio doesn't matter, but the principle does. Eventually we all get bored. Consequently, it is very important that you never do one thing for too long.

In the context of one working day, it is probably unhelpful for you to do one particular thing for more than a couple of hours. To stay fresh, you should move on to something else unless it is one of those exceptional items that simply has to be churned through from time to time and really does take a long while. Even then, you may still need regular breaks from it, and breaking up any monotonous task is a healthy thing to do.

In any particular working week, you really should not be doing literally the same thing every day. You can keep it up for a while, but not for months. Keep reminding yourself that *you* are the person in charge. Many who work on their own have deliberately left the strictures of company life precisely to gain greater freedom for themselves. It therefore represents a significant irony if they find that they are constrained in some way by their new circumstances. You may think that you *have* to do a certain thing, but there is always a chance that you do not. Simply pause to consider it, and if the job is really too horrible, decide whether to find a different way round it or, in extreme cases, whether to turn the task down.

In any working year, if your work is too repetitive, you have almost certainly got the mix wrong. You need to take time out to review what types of work make up your livelihood. Get a large piece of paper and jot down all the types of work you do. Now put a percentage of time spent by each of them. What does this tell you? For example, if you have only two categories on your sheet of paper, then this means that you spend *half a year* doing each. That sounds fairly dull, and if this is indeed the case, then you need to be utterly convinced that you love your subject matter and can keep your enthusiasm levels up every time you are engaged to do such jobs. Even if you have six things on the list, you will still have spent two months on each that year. Are you happy with that? If not, you need to re-engineer how you make your money by making some positive changes. Consider declining work that you have too much of, and finding new ways to stimulate more interesting things to do so that you can have a better mix.

If, when reviewing three years or more of the nature of your work, you conclude that you have been doing the same thing for too long, you have a serious problem. There's no point in embarking on the euphoria and pride of working on your own only to find that you have invented a new but equally boring mousetrap. It really is quite heartbreaking if someone who works on their own says that they are bored and have been for years. It doesn't make any sense at all. Their destiny is in their own hands, so unfortunately one can only conclude that someone who claims this is probably quite boring themselves and does not have the necessary enterprise to change what they do. You need to nip monotony in the bud.

All in all, regardless of what time period you are looking at, this mantra will serve you well:

If your work is becoming repetitive, change it.

86 Don't forget to build time off into your year plan

Staying sane and relentlessly enthusiastic. Mmm. Is this a realistic goal or some sort of nirvana that nobody who works on their own could realistically be expected to achieve? We'll have a look at the sanity part first.

The definition of sanity is 'the state of having a normal healthy mind' or 'good sense and soundness of judgement'.

> *'The definition of insanity is doing the same thing over and over again and expecting different results.'* (Benjamin Franklin)

We are talking here about the condition of a rational person who feels well balanced and reasonably calm. Many aspects of modern life would appear to be designed to unhinge us at every opportunity, and the pressures of any breadwinner in today's society are well documented. This is precisely why so many people choose to earn their living from a company rather than to generate the income themselves. They welcome the comfort and the safety net that company structures appear to offer. The buildings are provided and so is the pattern of work. Sometimes they receive all sorts of other luxuries – cars, travel allowances, health care, life insurance, and so on. And although it often appears that these parts of the package are there purely for their monetary value, in truth many people value them for their supporting properties as much as their financial value.

In some circles, this debate has moved on so far that you can now find books that ask what companies are for anyway. Some conclude that, whereas many would assume that they are there to make money for the owners, they actually perform a focal role in society and are there to bind people together in a structured way. We have all met people who claim that they couldn't get anything done if it weren't for their partner who organizes everything, whether that's arranging the social life, remembering birthdays or booking a holiday. In a work context, there would appear to be many who could not even do their work without the support services provided by their colleagues – the majority of these colleagues seemingly more junior than them. You know the sort of thing: 'If her secretary wasn't there she wouldn't turn up anywhere.'

You need to engineer a set-up that keeps you sane. How then, do you also remain relentlessly enthusiastic? First of all, enthusiasm is an absolutely fundamental prerequisite of someone who runs their own business. Nobody else is going to generate business for you. No one else is going to be enthusiastic on your behalf. The job falls to you. People don't want to do business with someone who lacks enthusiasm, so one way or another you need to find a way of having an endless supply of the stuff. In a way, that is what this whole book is about, and if you are looking for ideas, scan the 110-point guide at the back. However, roughly:

* Keep lots of variety in what you do to stay fresh
* Get keyed up for phone calls and meetings, and try to be in a good mood before you do them
* Change things if you don't find them interesting
* Take a sensible amount of time off so that you can return to your work energetically.

The net effect for your customers should be that your enthusiasm *appears* to be relentless even though of course it is impossible for any person to be in that state as a permanent condition. You will have noticed that a vital part of this is taking the right amount of time off work. How many times have you heard a self-employed person say that they haven't had a holiday for ages? Even if they have arranged it and left the country, they still keep worrying about the business when they are lying on a beach somewhere. This is a poor formula that usually leads to some form of meltdown, with both the business and the individual inevitably suffering.

One particularly helpful trick is to build time off into your plan for the year. Don't do it on the fly halfway through. If you do it ad hoc like this, there is a very strong chance that the break that you do go for won't really do the trick. You will almost certainly have compromised on one aspect or another, and this does not befit the reward that you have earned entirely off your own bat. So look at the year and ask yourself these sorts of questions:

- When are the best times of year to be away?
- Will you take one large chunk or several smaller bits?
- Do you need a sabbatical?
- If so, how would you arrange it?
- What if you plan a 10-month year instead of 12?
- Can you arrange the financial aspects now?
- Where do you want to go?
- In what sort of style?
- With anyone else or on your own?
- What sort of research do you need to do before you can answer some of these questions?

This way, you can plan excellent time off, pre-market the timing of it to your customers, and you do not need to worry about the possible implications when you are away because you have planned the whole thing properly. In addition, the fact that you have put so much thought into your recreational time says volumes about the level of thought that you apply to your customers' business issues. Even better, when you are actually taking the time off, you can relax completely safe in the knowledge that this is *exactly* what you have been working for.

87 When you take time off, be genuinely unavailable

What is the point of taking a break if you spend a vast amount of it checking messages on your mobile phone or logging on to your e-mail system? It is quite simple to put the measures in place to explain why you are not around before you make yourself unavailable. Also don't forget that corporate time moves differently to normal time, so many of your clients won't even notice that you have gone away anyway (see Chapter 6). Here is the self-employed person's guide to taking time off and being *genuinely* unavailable:

- Put your mobile phone in a drawer and under no circumstances take it with you
- Do not visit an internet café unless you have a burning need to contact a loved one (try postcards or a landline instead – they worked fine for years)
- Do not take any work material with you at all
- Change the messages on your phones to explain what is going on
- Set up an auto response on your e-mail to do the same

- Tell your customers a long way in advance that you will not be available (this often means that you actually receive significantly more work before you go so that their needs are covered whilst you are away).

All in all, this approach works really well. There will of course be some lines of work where you really do need to be contactable, but you can judge the level of that for yourself. Suffice to say that if you apply a fraction of the above, you will stand a better chance of having a decent break, and that will be in everybody's interests.

88 Develop new hobbies to alleviate monotony and make you more interesting

A topic related to taking time off is the development of hobbies. This is not so that you can spend weeks on end doing the hobby and not working, although there may be some cases whereby what starts life as a hobby purely for pleasure actually becomes income generating. But let's assume for the moment that it is solely for pleasure. What purpose do hobbies serve?

First of all, they have the capacity to alleviate monotony. Take a little break from time to time to do the thing that you want. It could be playing a musical instrument, reading, poetry, painting, sport – anything you like. They can all play an important role in adding variety to your day.

Second, they tend to make people more interesting by adding another dimension to what could otherwise be regarded as simply a 'business person'. The more obscure the hobby, the more interesting you become. This makes you more intriguing to talk to, and the fact that you do something constructive in your spare time says volumes about your level of application and your potential to deliver in a business context.

89 If you have had a good day, reward yourself

Do bear in mind that when you work on your own, the only person who can reward you is *you*. Naturally, the money you receive for your work is in itself a form of reward, but here we are referring to the more emotional side of things. Occasionally someone will thank you or say well done for something, and that is very nice in its own right. Yet sometimes you need to extend the courtesy to yourself. It's a good discipline because it forces you to review what has been achieved and then decide what level of reward is appropriate in return. Companies do it to their staff – now you need to learn how to do it for yourself.

For example, if you had set yourself a target of doing or achieving x, y and z in a day, and you find that you have done them all successfully (with the outcome you wanted) by lunchtime, consider taking the rest of the day off. Visit a museum, rearrange your wardrobe, go shopping, take a walk, whatever you fancy. Once you have got the hang of the idea, you can apply it to any time period you want:

If you have had a good week, reward yourself.

If you have had a good month, reward yourself.

If you have had a good year, reward yourself.

If you are the sort of person who likes targets as a motivational tool, you might want to fill in these headings and pin them to the wall:

My rewards

If I achieve _____ today,

I will reward myself with _____

_____

If I achieve _____ this week,

I will reward myself with _____

_____

If I achieve _____ this month,

I will reward myself with _____

_____

If I achieve _____ this year,

I will reward myself with _____

_____

---

90 Only over-deliver to a level that reflects your premium price

This is an issue that afflicts many people who run their own businesses. They are so desperate to please that they over-deliver hugely on every job. In the early days, this is reasonably understandable because every business needs a base from which to establish itself, and a job well done frequently leads to another. However, it is not a sustainable state of affairs in the long run. Why not? Because:

- Over-delivery equates to underpayment. Whichever way you look at it, you are being paid too little for doing too much.
- Work expands to fit the available time. If you haven't got enough to do then spend the spare time on getting more paid work, not doing more on the things for which you are already being paid (too little).
- After a while, your customers will become used to the level of service that the over-delivery represents. This is where it all starts to go wrong, and there are only two possible outcomes:
  1 They will not want you to put your prices up to reflect the time that you really are spending on their work
  2 The next time you do a job for them, they will expect the same level of over-delivery and will be upset if you do not deliver it.

Either way you are in an awkward position, so don't let it get to that stage. The moral is that you should only over-deliver to the point that reflects your pricing, preferably your premium pricing. This basically means that you should set a relatively high but fair price at the beginning of a job and it then becomes your decision whether to eat into some of your own margin to increase the amount of service you eventually provide. In the end everybody wins with this approach because you have commanded a good price and your customer has had excellent delivery.

91 Get your working environment right

One final point with regard to staying sane and enthusiastic: you can't do it if you don't like your working environment.

Given that running your own business is a daily process of motivation and reinvention, you cannot hope to achieve this if you don't like where you work. If you work at home, there are all sorts of things that you can do to get comfortable:

- Some people like to have a clearly differentiated room to work in where they can spread out, have all their stuff, and generally make a mess. Others only need a desk in the corner of the bedroom. Work out your preferred style.
- Decide on the level of tidiness you require about the place and arrange things accordingly.
- If you have a partner or other family members around you at home, talk to them about the bits that matter to you. What is out of bounds? Which things do you use in a working context that are in the house? Are there any aspects of other people's clutter and behaviour that prevent you from getting things done? If so, have you found a polite way of discussing it? Once you have mentioned it, they can understand better that the home is also a working environment, and perhaps make a few adjustments to help.

Some people simply cannot work at home. Even though they can work effectively on their own, they require the discipline of a separate place of work to get them in the mood. These types should consider:

- Does the place that I work in really reflect my style?
- Is my journey to work sensible or is it just as bad as travelling to a company?
- Do I get to fraternize with like-minded people, or would I be better off somewhere else?

One way or another, you need to be inspired to get your work done: if your environment isn't right, change it.

So there we have it. Take the work seriously, but not yourself. Don't do the same thing for too long, and take sensible time off, preferably to do something really stimulating. Throw some hobbies into the mix, rather than over-deliver when you aren't being paid enough to justify it. This all adds up to a decent balance that will make you better at everything you do.

Which, of course, will certainly increase your chances of staying sane and appearing, or even truly being, relentlessly enthusiastic.

Cautionary Tale: Fiona Flatter, Public Relations Consultant

Many PR people are renowned for their enthusiasm, but there is a big difference between appearing to be enthusiastic with clients, and being truly motivated yourself. Fiona usually came across as keen, but by the end of her first two years' flying solo, she was getting really bored. So what went wrong?

Fiona's first mistake was to take herself too seriously. It's all very well to be top dog in a company and wallow in all the support facilities, but when you work on your own there aren't any. She was also quite one-dimensional in a business sense. In her previous life, she had been very good at just one type of public relations. On her own, this rather narrow offering of only one specialism did not create as much variety as a generalist approach might have done. It also led to boredom, because the subject matter and the techniques were always the same.

Frustration bred desperation, and the work, although unfulfilling, became all-consuming. She didn't take much time off. She sidelined her hobbies, and failed to find a way of rewarding herself even when she had actually made good progress. Her office was an uninspiring mess that she regularly failed to tidy, so her shabby working environment began to reflect her state of mind. She became an example of someone who was a success technically, but who wasn't enjoying it.

Fiona's public relations were better than her relationship with herself.

Chapter 9 Staying sane and relentlessly enthusiastic

Checklist: what have you done? ✓

1 Taken the issues seriously, but not yourself ☐

2 Never done one thing for too long ☐

3 Not forgotten to build time off into your year plan ☐

4 Taken time off, and been genuinely unavailable ☐

5 Developed new hobbies to alleviate monotony and make you more interesting ☐

6 If you had a good day, rewarded yourself ☐

7 Only over-delivered to a level that reflects your premium price ☐

8 Got your working environment right ☐

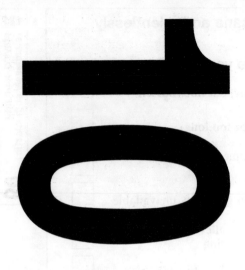

10

you are not alone

In this chapter you will learn
- how to establish your own self-employed network
- how to say no politely
- how to refer your surplus work to others
- how to enjoy the camaraderie of other companies
- how to blur the lines between work and social life

Here's an old joke you might enjoy. Three monks are sitting in the desert having taken a lifelong vow of silence. As they sit there in total tranquillity, a small cloud of dust gathers far off on the horizon. After staring at it for seven years, the first monk turns to the one in the middle and says: 'What's that?'

Seven years later, after no little analysis, the second monk replies: 'I think it's a horse.'

Seven years after that, the third monk rounds on the other two, exclaiming: 'It's too bloody noisy here. I'm off!'

Which just goes to show that peace and quiet is a very relative state of affairs. Or, to put it another way, two people are placed on top of two different mountains. One thinks it's a disaster because they can't talk to anyone, the other thinks 'Peace at last'. You get the idea.

92 Just because you work on your own, it doesn't mean you *are* alone

Feeling alone is a state of mind.

One person might be happy seeing one other person a day. Another might find that intolerable, and require the company of twenty. It rather depends on what you have to do with your time and how needy you are when it comes to interacting with other people. The trick is to keep your head steady and gradually to engineer the pattern of your day, week or month into something that you actively enjoy.

Remember that lots of people are full of admiration for the fact that you work on your own in the first place. They may well envy your ability to go to the shops when you like, declare your own day off from time to time, and not be ordered around by a boss that you may or may not respect. So when you feel a bit isolated, just remind yourself that it is your decision what you do next. It is your choice to decide how often you wish to be 'alone', what to do with any spare time, and how to use it to relax on your own terms, or to contact someone you want.

If someone has lots of friends but happens not to be in anyone's company at a particular moment, to what extent are they 'alone'? For every sole trader who wants to meet more people, there are hundreds of employees in companies yearning for everyone else to go away so that they can get on with their own thing. So the knack is to work out, understand, and appreciate all the contacts you have, and all the opportunities there are for interaction with those people, and organize the shape of it to suit your particular preference. These days, this set of interrelationships would probably be called a network.

93 Establish your own self-employed network

What is a network anyway? It isn't tangible, so if it does exist, it exists in your mind as a set of contacts organized along whatever lines suit you. Or it may not be organized at all, although when you work on your own that may be a bit too random for your own good. So if you can have a network when you work for a company, and in your social life, then you can certainly have one when you work for yourself.

One crucial thing links everyone who works on their own: they work on their own!

Which means that they all go through what you go through. There are few more unifying features than this one crucial bit of common ground. So whenever self-employed people meet, they usually end up with lots to discuss. The sort of stuff they talk about is often very wide-ranging, precisely because they are juggling all the work and personal issues that this book raises. This may sound self-evident, but consider the number of business meetings between those who work for companies that never get near to touching on their feelings or social lives – the things that *really* matter to them. There are millions of these so-called conversations everyday, and they are usually much more one-dimensional than the subject matter when two sole traders meet.

So the conversations between sole traders are wider ranging and have a tremendous capacity to generate genuine empathy. Put simply: you are very likely to sympathize with each other and to get on. That's a good basis for a relationship. You will both want to pay significant attention to what the other is good at, and what they enjoy doing. This makes sense for three reasons:

- You are in the same boat
- You both earn a living by listening to others
- They might be able to help you (the other person will be thinking the same thing).

That's a good equation in anyone's book. If this state of affairs is repeated over multiple conversations for a year or two, you are going to develop a pretty extensive set of contacts with other sole traders with whom you can swap experiences and other contacts. This applies whether they work in your area or not. Those who do similar work to you will be interesting to meet because you can compare specifics about your field, and they may be very useful to know about when it comes to referring surplus work (see later in this chapter). Self-employed people who do not work in your sector are equally fascinating to talk to. As well as all the general issues that confront those who work on their own, you may well find that it is their very lack of knowledge about your area that makes their comments all the more valuable. You have all heard people say 'I'm too close to it', so this type of encounter offers the equivalent of an objective commentator whose opinions are not biased by what they think they already know about your subject.

So now you have a self-employed network.

94 Balance the service equation

Over service or service over?

We have already discussed one of the most difficult juggling acts that the sole trader has to carry off. At one end of the spectrum you need to know how to fill in time when you don't have enough work, and at the other you have to work out how to behave when you can't fit it all in. Either extreme is dangerous if not handled sensitively. In Chapter 9 we looked at the economic implications of this ('Only over-deliver to a level that reflects your premium price', p.118). But here we are concerned with those aspects that affect your state of mind.

Take a look at the diagram on the next page.

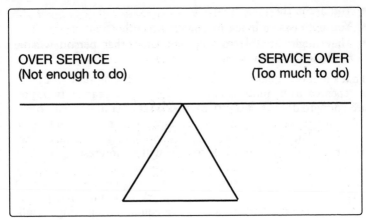

OVER SERVICE
(Not enough to do)

SERVICE OVER
(Too much to do)

Balancing the service equation

Let's look at the over-servicing end first. If you are over-servicing a customer, it may well be because you have spotted a future opportunity and wish to demonstrate a point, or just that you like the work, or the customer. However, there is also a chance that you are doing it because you are filling in the time to ensure that you have plenty of interaction with others. Or, put more bluntly, to stop yourself from being lonely. This isn't a great thing to do. What is happening here is that you are usurping your business requirements with your personal emotional needs. A well-balanced interlocking of the two is a good thing. Using your business as an emotional crutch is not.

So pause to consider whether you are using your business too much to support your emotional needs.

If you are, then change the balance, because you can be sure that fairly soon your customers will begin to notice too. That means that they will realize that you are actually not that busy (which will make them question why you are not much in demand), or they will get used to your being constantly available for their every demand (which you will regret later when you do have a lot to do). Either way, you will be creating a situation that is not in your favour.

Now let's look at the 'service over' end. What does it mean? It means that the service you provide is over because you cannot provide what the customer is asking for at the time they want it. Some sole traders go into a flat spin when this happens. Some over promise. Some fudge it. Good ones turn it to their advantage. Does the fact that you cannot do the job *precisely* when they need it this time mean that they will never be a customer again? Not necessarily. The knack is to work out how to say no politely, and there are lots of ways of doing it.

95 Learn to say no politely

People often feel that if they say no, then that's the end of it, and that the person asking the question will end up being annoyed. This doesn't have to be the case. Let's have a look at some of the circumstances in which you might not be able to agree to a customer request:

- you haven't got the time
- the price isn't right
- the type of work isn't quite what you like
- you have done so much of the same work recently that you would rather do something else
- you did not enjoy working with them before and would rather not again.

The precise reasons don't really matter. The point is that you need to explain your position in a way that leaves the door open for further business in due course should things change. Why is that? Because at some point in the future:

- you may well have the time
- the price might well be right
- the nature of the request from that person may be different
- you may not have done that type of work for a while
- your opinion of the customer may have changed.

Everything is constantly changing, and it changes faster when you work on your own than it does in a company. So stay open-minded and let them down politely and gently.

Here are some civilized ways of declining work and some possible reactions.

> *I'm really sorry, I am fully booked at the moment. Can the deadline be moved back at all?*

A lot of customers respect the fact that you are busy. It proves that you are successful and in demand, and it reflects and confirms the value of your premium pricing. Anyway, time might not be their main consideration. There will be those that get the hump, but they often come back at a later date, particularly if they have a less than satisfactory experience elsewhere (which they often do, particularly if they go for a 'quick fix' alternative).

I'm really sorry, I have just completed a massive programme of exactly that sort of work, and I have decided to take a breather from it before taking on any more.

Customers always want people to be fresh and keen on their subject matter, so your reaction is honest and reasonable. It might not suit their immediate needs, but it is representative of a respectful attitude. They might not like it, but then again they may come back to you later with requests for different types of work that you would enjoy more.

I'm really sorry, I am fully booked at the moment. May I refer you to someone else who does the same sort of work, who may be able to do it for you? I know them well and think they would offer a suitable alternative.

This is a very constructive response, and they will probably thank you for it because it is a very professional thing to do. It proves that you are 'big' enough to pass work on. It also shows that you have a good working knowledge of your market to go with your magnanimous attitude. The contact you refer them to will certainly thank you too (see next section). If you are incredibly unlucky, they will commission your contact to do the work, prefer them to you, and give them all their future work. So you will have lost a customer. But that's pretty unlikely. Now read on.

96 Refer your surplus work to others

How would you feel if the phone rang and there was someone on the line offering you work? Not a full-time job, you understand, just a really decent project of the type where you usually have to invest a lot of time to secure it. This time, the pre-sale work has all been done, and they are offering it to you. There could be lots of reasons. They are too busy to do it themselves. They are going on holiday. They were asked about it, but it isn't precisely what they are best at. So they call to ask if you would be interested.

It's a great feeling, and it happens when you have let other sole traders know what you do, and when you have offered to help them if they ever get stuck. It works both ways. You may well have been in the same position yourself and referred some work to them some time in the past. Whatever the reason, it is one of the most cost-effective calls you will ever receive, apart from a dream customer ringing out of the blue precisely when you want, proposing exactly what you like, at the right price.

So this is a 'golden phone call', and they really can work in both directions. You are not alone as a sole trader precisely because these calls move back and forth between well-connected self-employed people all the time. They come about because you have presented your skills well, been thoughtful in introducing contacts to each other, and probably because you have already generated business for the person who is calling you now. Even better, these calls are completely free. They involve none of the usual investment of time and effort that most new business pursuits do. And once you have set the ball rolling, they start working their way back to you.

Sometimes these interrelationships can progress a step further by turning into proper working alliances and subcontracting arrangements. This can be good or bad, depending on how you handle things. Having an overflow facility for your business is good, and so is picking up work from contacts when you have not had to over-invest in securing it. On the downside, these arrangements can take a lot of time and maintenance, so you have to keep a very close eye on whether they are taking up too much of your time in relation to the work they actually generate. The self-employed world is littered with examples of people who talk a good game about networks and alliances, but when you dig deeper you often find that they spend too much time feeding the arrangement to justify the negligible amount of work that it creates. By all means develop your contacts, but don't fall into this trap.

97 Enjoy the camaraderie of other companies

Here's another very good reason why you are not alone. We have already looked at how you can generate a culture even when you work on your own (Chapter 7, 'You are the company culture'). So it stands to reason that a company with two or more people in it will also have its own culture. This usually happens the moment those two people decide to take a break and go to the pub. By the time there is a full payroll, all sorts of social activities start to develop. Banter in reception. Jokes around the coffee machine. A quick drink after work. Sporting challenges. Mutual hobbies. The bigger the company, the more there is of it. And chances are that many of your customers are just such companies. Which means that there is a hybrid of business and social life waiting out there for you to join when you need it.

In other words, not all of your entertainment has to be generated by you. Although as a sole trader you will become a master of creating almost everything yourself, this does not necessarily have to apply to the human company that you may need in order to stay sane (we came up with enough of these in the last chapter). There are actually hundreds of enjoyable opportunities lurking within many of your customer relationships, so it is your job to work out what type and frequency of interaction provides you with the right balance. Chances are that these social interactions will have a positive bonding effect on your customer relationships too.

Just a couple of words of warning though: under no circumstances allow yourself to become known as a party freeloader. This advice is not an excuse to gatecrash scores of customer parties and gain a reputation for coasting on their hospitality. Use your judgement to join in with those activities that you enjoy, and which are appropriate in the context of your business relationship with the customer.

98 Blur the lines between work and social life

Is it likely that self-employed people generate a lot of business out of social situations? Certainly. In fact, one of the main points about working for yourself is that there should be less of a distinction between work and social life. The old-fashioned lines of demarcation between work and play should become more vague as your solo life becomes more established. You know the sort of thing that represents a regimented life: alarm goes, leave home, use public transport, enter place of work, begin work. Do the whole thing in reverse at the end of the day. Begin social life.

This is precisely what you left a company to avoid, or why you never joined one in the first place. So it doesn't make much sense to set up a whole new set of equally pointless boundaries in your new life. We have discussed some of these parameters already. 'Introduce some humanity into your CV' in Chapter 4 was all about laying the ground for a respectful interplay between your private and business life. 'Develop new hobbies to alleviate monotony and make you more interesting' in Chapter 9 was all about broadening your appeal by diversifying your interests so that they imply how sharp you are as a business person. Here, we are going one step further and blurring the lines between work and social life.

We already know that you can't permanently be in work mode, but equally of course you can't be in constant play mode either. However, what you can do is take a more relaxed view about whether you are 'on duty' or not. This does not cut only in favour of relaxing more. It also means that when you are socializing, you may equally be 'working'. The balance you create here is really important. It doesn't have to be arduous either way. That's why you need to have your antenna scanning for work opportunities, common areas, contacts, ideas, and so on, but all in a relaxed social context. Don't force it or get uptight. Keep it loose and stay open-minded.

You really never do know when an amazing opportunity is lurking in the next enjoyable night out.

99 View it like an extended family

How often do you see the members of your family? The answer to this question varies enormously by individual. Some people live next door to their family members and see them all the time. Some have emigrated and are lucky to see them once a year. Somewhere in the middle lies a mixture of contact points and frequencies that the family members work out amongst themselves. You will know roughly how often you speak to your parents, siblings, grandparents, cousins, and so on, and in return, so will they.

Your business contacts can be viewed in exactly the same way so that you can judge the appropriate frequency that suits the relationship. Once you have thought about this, you will have unwittingly designed a latticework of contact points that prove conclusively that you are not alone. If you remain uncertain, do the old trick of writing it down. The proof will be there in front of you.

The family analogy may also help you to classify some of your contacts. Who are the 'must call once a week' customers? Who are the less well-known relations who are happy to chat once every few months? Once you get the hang of it, you can extend the metaphor from phone calls to meetings, anniversaries, parties – pretty much any interaction that has a bearing on the business but that can spill into a social setting.

100 If you stay in touch, they will too

As with all pieces of general advice, this assertion is only half true. Although there are always some people in the world who never seem to return calls, cards or invitations, most people do. If you really do have some hopeless contacts that never get in touch, then you should seriously consider whether they are worth staying in touch with at all. Think about it. If they don't call back, then you are clearly not doing business together. If that is consistently the case, then why bother with these people? We examined in Chapter 5, 'Taming the telephone', what to do if potential customers refuse to take your calls and concluded that, even if they eventually did, they would probably be a nightmare to deal with anyway. So you can cut out a lot of soul-destroying heartache if you weed out such contacts.

But let's be more optimistic and assume that most right-minded people do stay in touch. Once you get rolling with your 'keep in touch' programme, it will start to generate contacts in return without you actually doing anything. You will soon discover that you are not the sole initiator of an outbound contact programme. Don't forget that other people will be doing exactly the same thing. And don't forget the first point in this book: *Assume that you have something to offer.*

The number of people with whom you stay in touch, and the frequency with which you do so, is critical. We looked at the business implications of this balance in Chapter 2, 'The right tools for the job', and we introduced the idea of the Pester Line to prevent you from irritating potential customers unduly. But here we are interested in the other side of the equation. You must not fritter away your energy by frequently contacting people who won't keep in touch with you in return. It's a total waste of your time, and that ultimately means money. So it is important that you review regularly the people with whom you stay in touch, and whether it is worth your while. At the beginning, you need to develop an initial pool of contacts, and of course until you have attempted to stay in touch with someone for a reasonable period, you won't know what their track record is in this department. But as soon as you realize that they never really bother to stay in touch and so do not represent any kind of business opportunity, then you need seriously to consider whether they should be dropped from your Contact List.

101 One man's solitary confinement is another man's freedom

So do you really still think that you are alone? One would hope by now that you don't really believe it, but let's finally nail the point anyway. Solitary confinement is one way of viewing self-employment, and splendid isolation is another. It all depends on your perspective. It doesn't take a genius to work out that the successful sole trader will choose to see it as the latter. Now that you work on your own, your job is to be an optimistic self-starter. You are free to do what you like, when you like. You are not in the slightest bit alone. In fact, there is a strong chance that you lead a far less isolated life than many of those who mingle with hundreds of people every day. That's because you are doing it on your terms.

Never forget why you first went self-employed or why you are seriously considering it now. You want to do things your way. That means you are in charge. You decide how much thinking time you need. How much peace and quiet. How much action. And how much interaction. You can meet as many people as you like, or as few. You can have hugely socially interactive days, and really quiet, peaceful ones. You can mix them up to your liking. It's great! There are people in corporations all over the world who would be highly envious of that level of freedom. So make it work for you, and enjoy it.

Chapter 10 You are not alone

Checklist: what have you done? ✓

1 Accepted that, although you work on your own, you are not alone

2 Established your own self-employed network

3 Balanced the service equation

4 Learned to say no politely

5 Referred your surplus work to others

6 Enjoyed the camaraderie of other companies

7 Blurred the lines between work and social life

8 Viewed it like an extended family

9 Stayed in touch, so they will too

10 Chosen your opinion: solitary confinement or freedom

11 how looking back helps you to look forward

In this chapter you will learn
- how to review your business historically
- how to work out whether what you do is okay
- how to change your business if you conclude that it isn't okay
- to develop the knack of working out whether something is a waste of time
- more advice on self-motivation

Being retrospective doesn't mean losing perspective. Considering the past doesn't necessarily mean indulging in nostalgia. In fact, many people who work on their own repeat their mistakes precisely because they *don't* review the past and learn anything from it. Assume looking back will be a positive process, and read on.

102 Look back at all the customers you have worked for and your work for them

Every now and then you need to pause and reflect. Look back over what you have done and ask yourself one of your most powerful questions:

What does that tell me?

The frequency with which you should do this rather depends on the nature of your business. Once a year is essential, but if you operate in a market that has particular seasons or phases, or certain cornerstone events or moments in time, it may be useful to do it more often.

In general, looking back is not deemed to be helpful for moving forward, yet reviewing the past objectively can give you some fantastic ideas and insights, based on what you have already done. Large organizations have data and records to draw on, but when you run your own business you tend to have a very limited amount of that sort of information. In reality, most of it will probably be in your head. Start by jotting down the overall shape of your business:

- What was your total income last year?
- What were your costs?
- What was your profit?
- How many customers did you have?
- How many jobs or transactions did you complete?
- What was the highest value transaction?
- What was the lowest?
- What was the average?
- What was the average value of a customer?
- How does this compare with the year(s) before?

You can do this on one or two sheets of paper, and it gives you a basic overview. You should end up with a shape a bit like this:

Year	Income	Jobs	Customers	Repeat	%	Cost per job	Value per customer
2000	£98,000	17	7	10	58	£5,700	£14,000
2001	£104,000	16	12	9	56	£6,500	£8,600
2002	£105,000	37	18	21	56	£2,800	£5,800
2003	£150,000	45	10	38	84	£3,300	£15,000
2004	£200,000	45	10	40	88	£4,500	£20,000

Year on year trading comparison

If you are summarizing this snapshot to a friend, you need to be able to clearly answer the questions:

- Is the business going up or down?
- Is the customer mix right?
- Is the number of transactions per customer appropriate?
- Is the level of repeat purchase acceptable?
- Is the cost per job viable?
- Is the value per customer adequate?
- What are the important things that need to change?
- Can you cope with the general shape of all this?

Anyone who runs their own business needs to have a firm and up-to-date grip on these matters. As a rough rule of thumb, if you can't rattle off these details on request at any moment of the day, then you aren't sufficiently on top of your business.

103 If something you offer is very popular, work out why

Now start to look at the nature of the work you have carried out in the recent past. Differentiate between tasks, and group them.

- What did you do most of?
- What did you do the least?
- How many types of work do you do?
- Are some types more viable than others?
- Are some more enjoyable than others?

- Is anything in particular especially popular with your customers?
- Is it the same thing that you enjoy most?
- Could it be?

Answering these questions could help you to re-engineer your business on your own terms. If the things you enjoy most make the most money, then you are in luck (or you are a master of balancing work and pleasure). If not, consider whether you can change the proportion of less enjoyable and lower margin jobs for ones that make better economic and pleasure sense. You really do owe this to yourself. Do remember that there is no point in standing at a bar moaning about the shape of your business, because the shape of your business is entirely down to you (we covered this in Chapter 7, 'Never moan', p.90). Over a reasonable period of time, after you have done all the hard work of setting up and compromising on one or two early jobs to get the business going, you really should be able to arrange this money–enjoyment balance more to your liking.

104 If something you offer doesn't generate enough profit, work out why

The flip side of this exercise is to identify things that you sell or do that actually don't make much money. It is extraordinary how many businesses produce huge quantities of work or product in a particular area only to conclude that it is neither viable nor that enjoyable to do. This is why regular reviews are important, otherwise you could be continuing indefinitely wasting your time on something that you don't necessarily like doing, and which doesn't even bring in worthwhile money.

Be honest with yourself. If something you offer doesn't make enough money, work out why and make the necessary decisions.

- What would happen if you stopped doing that thing?
- Would the business suffer in any way?
- Would more time be released for you to do more enjoyable or profitable things?
- Would anyone notice or care?
- Would the quality of your working life improve?
- Would the quality of your personal life improve?

Sweep up this information and change the elements that don't work. It will be a cathartic and rejuvenating exercise.

105 Think of everything that is similar to what you do and consider whether to do that as well

139 how looking back helps you to look forward 11

Write down in one sentence precisely what you do for a living and how you make your money. Sounds simple? There are thousands of people who find this a really difficult thing to do. Whether this is because they are used to waffling or are permanently afraid to come to the point, we'll never know. But assuming that you have succeeded, now start writing next to your one sentence things that are similar in nature.

- Does the thing that you do or sell have similarities with other markets or products?
- If so, which ones?
- Could you extend your business into those areas?
- Does the manner in which you provide a product or service have parallels with other markets?
- Which ones?
- Could you use the same principles to diversify what you do?

If the answer is yes to any of these questions, it does not necessarily mean that you have automatically written the next phase of your business plan. Against any area where you have answered yes, you now need to ask yourself:

'Would I enjoy doing that?'

If the answer is again yes, then you can certainly start to investigate the viability of the potential new area. It is of course quite possible that, although there are indeed similarities between your skills and the new area under consideration, the other area will not make you money for reasons that are unrelated to your existing sphere of business. If that is the case, you now need to weigh up whether the potential enjoyment of this new area is sufficient to offset the financial paucity of the opportunity.

There is nothing wrong with pursuing a low margin opportunity provided that you know exactly why you are doing it. Possible reasons might include:

- Your are happy to do it for the satisfaction alone
- You have never done it before and you want to learn how
- It's a good cause that you care a lot about
- You don't need the money.

106 Describe your business to a respected friend and listen to what they say

From time to time it is a great discipline to describe your business to a friend. It is not important whether they know anything about your line of work or not (in fact, it is often very helpful if they don't), but it does matter that they are fairly switched on and that they have a good track record of telling you the truth even if it may be a bit unpalatable sometimes. Tell them in layman's terms what you do all day and how you make your money. Keep it simple and don't use any jargon. That way, they will be able to judge your business on first principles: what you do, who buys it, and how you make a profit on the way.

During this type of conversation it is almost always the case that the other person will come up with a blindingly obvious question or observation that you hadn't considered. It isn't entirely clear why this tends to happen, but it may be something to do with the fact that you do a lot of things instinctively, and that you are usually too busy to stop and contemplate what you are doing. It sounds a bit odd, but it really does work.

Pay attention to what they say and decide whether there is any course of action that would be appropriate as a result. Sometimes the obvious things are the best. In truth, when you work on your own, they almost always are.

107 Pretend you couldn't work for six months: what would you do?

This is an interesting exercise that is particularly helpful if you have the general feeling that you don't really enjoy the bulk of what you do all day. Take a moment to imagine what you would do if you couldn't work for six months. The hypothetical reason for not being able to work doesn't really matter – it could be injury, collapse of your business, collapse of you personally, unforeseen personal circumstances, a sabbatical, anything you like. Now: what on earth would you do with yourself?

Before you conclude that this is a complete waste of time and too fanciful, do remind yourself of the fundamental principle behind working on your own: the reason you do it is to create as good a balance as possible between your business and your personal life. Therefore, it makes sense that wherever possible the one should compliment the other. Which means that as often as possible the nature of the work that earns you money should also give you enjoyment.

So now write down everything that you would do with your six months off. When you have the complete list, go back through it and work out whether any of these things offer any earning potential. Is there a market for them, and could you make money out of your enjoyment? This is the first step towards achieving the ultimate nirvana of being paid for something you enjoy. Review your passions, and see if you can convert them into earning potential.

108 Develop the knack of working out whether something is a waste of time

Isn't it easy to get all excited about something, rush off and dive into it, and not realize until much later that it was a total waste of time? That's true generally in life, and it certainly applies to business. If you work for a company, or if you are the sort of person who likes to follow a whim and dabble in a project without minding if you drop it quite quickly, then it doesn't really cause much harm. But if you work on your own, this whole process can have a devastating effect. If you go haring off in a certain direction without pausing to answer some basic questions and learn some simple lessons, you will have unwittingly developed the habit of frittering away your time and not making any decent money.

You need to develop the knack of working out whether something is going to be a waste of time, before you get in too deep. If this does not come naturally to you, one thing that can really help is to look back over any false starts and dead-end projects from the past so that you can work out precisely why they didn't work out. Work back through your leads and remind yourself of all the things that *didn't* come to fruition. This isn't usually as easy as reviewing the actual business that you have done because most people don't keep any record of what didn't happen. Nevertheless, with a little contemplation you can usually piece together the ones that got away. You might need a few hours quietly reflecting, or you might want to sit down with a glass of wine away from the hurly-burly of a normal working day.

When you have drawn up the list, analyse it with these sorts of questions:

- Are there many missed opportunities on it?
- If so, what amount of business do they represent?
- How does the lost business compare with the amount of business that you actually did complete during the same time period?
- Is that an uncomfortable realization or are you happy with the ratio between the real and unrealized business?

Now take the list and start categorizing the types of business that didn't materialize:

- Was it lucrative?
- Was it interesting?
- Did you really want it?
- What would have happened if you had got the work?

From these lines of enquiry you can begin to work out why you didn't succeed in certain areas and whether it matters or not. This is the crucial part. There is no point in ruing the fact that you didn't get a particular bit of business when on reflection it would have radically altered the shape of your total business for the worse. If it was very valuable but would have put an unbearable strain on you, would you really have wanted it?

These are important things to discover because they become pieces of learning that can help you to shape your plans for the next year. Putting shape to your business is essential. There's nothing worse than someone who works on their own and doesn't really have any clear idea of what they would like to happen next. We are not talking here about massive away-days and spreadsheets and diagrams. Just a confident, thoughtful individual who can articulate what they do, and where they are heading. Such an individual is far more impressive than an employee who is simply repeating the company mission statement. It's an important knack to develop and a great feeling when you've got the hang of it. So make sure you can.

109 Resurrect something you used to enjoy doing

Much can fall by the wayside when you start your working life for a company, and it sometimes gets even worse when you start working on your own. This is not a desirable state of affairs. In fact, the whole point of being your own boss is to generate a good balance between the things that earn you a living and the things that you really like doing. Try this little exercise. Get a piece of paper and a cup of coffee, or whatever your particular poison is, and write down all the things that you really love doing. Now work back to your youth and think of anything that you used to like doing, but no longer do. A sport? Something artistic? An academic subject? Theatre? You get the idea.

Try to remember what it was about this pastime that captured your imagination. How do you feel about it now? Is the interest still there? Has it developed into something else? Would you like to do it again? If so, how would you set about it? Is there any relationship between that thing and the type of work that you now do to earn a living? If so, could they become one and the same thing?

By asking these seemingly never-ending chains of questions, you do eventually get to the bottom of whether you have any unfulfilled needs. This is not a deeply spiritual exercise, merely a good way of increasing your chances of answering the one question which vexes most people when it comes to their job:

'I don't really know what I want to do.'

110 Remember: everything you achieve, you have done yourself

By now you should be able to see how looking back can indeed help you to look forward. You should also have a fairly comprehensive picture of the sort of mental qualities needed to run your own business. You need to be a self-starter and very good at getting things done. You need to develop an appropriate level of confidence that stands you in good stead but does not spill over into arrogance. Self-motivation needs to come naturally, or at least be worked on until it becomes a quality that you can call upon when appropriate. You need to work out how to reward yourself in every sense – the money, the time off, and a healthy dose of mental adulation that reminds you that you do actually have some outstanding qualities, and have achieved some excellent things.

Because when you work on your own, there is one thing that no one can ever deny:

Everything you achieve, you have done yourself.

Off you go then, and good luck.

Success Story: Ruth Starr, Fashion Jeweller

Ruth sourced fashion jewellery from around the world, and was really good at re-inventing herself and her business. Everyone knows that fashion moves fast, so what's in today is out tomorrow. Ruth knew that her customer relationships were only as good as her next set of ideas and her next deal, and she worked very hard to stay ahead of the game.

Part of her approach was to review constantly what she had done before. This revealed all sorts of helpful things: how fashion tended to move in cycles, what the long-term re-ordering patterns of her biggest clients were, why things were popular and when they would be at their peak. She used this accumulated and regularly updated knowledge to influence her customers and to inform her next purchasing decisions.

She was forever thinking laterally about her business. A modest start in earrings turned into a host of other accessories – belts, handbags, hats and sunglasses. She was also clinical when it came to admitting that something hadn't worked. Instead of repeating her mistakes, she acknowledged them and moved on.

Ruth knew that looking back helps you to look forward, and she lived up to her name.

Chapter 11 How looking back helps you to look forward

Checklist: what have you done? ✓

1 Looked back at all the customers you have worked for and your work for them ☐

2 If something you offer is very popular, worked out why ☐

3 If something you offer doesn't generate enough profit, worked out why ☐

4 Thought of everything that is similar to what you do and considered whether to do that as well ☐

5 Described your business to a respected friend and listened to what they said ☐

6 Pretended you couldn't work for six months: what would you do? ☐

7 Developed the knack of working out whether something is a waste of time ☐

8 Resurrected something you used to enjoy doing ☐

9 Remembered: everything you achieve, you have done yourself ☐

appendices

This book has intentionally been kept to a manageable size because you will want to get through as much advice as you can in as little time as possible. In the same way, many people find it easier to digest and retain information if they can have it in bite-sized chunks. Consequently, the appendices contain a quick ten-point guide to running your own business, and all of the ideas in the book in one 110-point list. The ten-point list in Appendix 1 is very brief but is useful as an overview, and if you can hit nine out of ten in any given working week, you will definitely be a great success and a well-balanced individual. The 110-point list in Appendix 2 is much more a matter of personal choice. You will probably want to cherry pick the bits you like best to create your own credo.

Appendix 1

The quick ten-point guide to running your own business

1 Assume that you have something to offer

2 Take the issues seriously, but not yourself

3 Sell yourself, rather than materials with a mark-up

4 Charge a premium price and do a great job

5 Remember that corporate time moves slower than normal time

6 Listen more than you talk

7 Be more positive than everyone else wherever you go

8 Do not distinguish between nice and nasty things to do

9 Whatever you plan to do, start now

10 Remember: everything you achieve, you have done yourself

Appendix 2

The 110-point guide to running your own business

Chapter 1 Where do I start?
1 Assume that you have something to offer
2 Be honest with yourself
3 Research your market thoroughly
4 Work out how much money you need
5 Write a simple, realistic plan
6 Invest in a distinctive identity
7 Get connected
8 Appoint a good accountant
9 Work out the materials you need
10 Network constantly without being irritating
11 Now make it happen

Chapter 2 The right tools for the job
12 Write out your contact list and new business hit list
13 Write down everyone you want to get in touch with
14 Put the phone number by every one of your contacts
15 Do everything when you think of it, otherwise nothing will happen
16 Constantly review the new business hit list to see if you are being realistic
17 Keep the numbers manageable
18 Keep inventing new ideas for contacting someone
19 Every time you get through to someone, move them to your contact list
20 Try to have 20–30 meetings fixed for the next 4–6 weeks
21 Never cancel a new business meeting because you are 'too busy'

Chapter 3 Getting the money right
22 Concentrate on the money, but don't become obsessed with it
23 Weigh up the service vs product distinction
24 Work out how to have a near-infinite margin
25 Consider the lucky seven money questions
26 Try to avoid the most time-consuming issue ever: other people
27 Try to sell what you do, not materials with a mark-up
28 The price–quality equation: if you cost a lot, you must be good

Chapter 7 How to conduct yourself

61 You *are* the company culture
62 Only do business with people that you like
63 Subsume your ego
64 Do not distinguish between nice and nasty things to do
65 Talk to yourself
66 Remind yourself of all the positive things you have done
67 Never moan
68 Never drink during the day
69 Never watch daytime TV
70 Never finish a day before deciding what to do the next morning
71 Never do anything unless you know why you are doing it
72 Have reserve plans for every day
73 Remember that Plan B is often more productive than Plan A

Chapter 8 Meetings can be fun

74 When you secure a meeting, get organized straightaway
75 Get chronological
76 Research everything thoroughly
77 Give the client a list of ways in which you can help
78 Include things that you *could* do, even if you have never done them
79 Ask what is on the client's mind at the moment and offer to fix it
80 Listen more than you talk
81 Be more positive than everyone else in every meeting
82 Never be late
83 Be spontaneous and act naturally

Chapter 9 Staying sane and relentlessly enthusiastic

84 Take the issues seriously, but not yourself
85 Never do one thing for too long
86 Don't forget to build time off into your year plan
87 When you take time off, be genuinely unavailable
88 Develop new hobbies to alleviate monotony and make you more interesting
89 If you have had a good day, reward yourself
90 Only over-deliver to a level that reflects your premium price
91 Get your working environment right

Chapter 10 You are not alone

Chapter 11 How looking back helps you to look forward

Helpful sources of information

Institute of Business Advisers: **www.iba.org.uk**
Company registrations: **www.companieshouse.gov.uk**
Department of Trade and Industry: **www.dti.gov.uk**
Business Hotline Publications:
www.businesshotlinepublications.co.uk

Further reading

Teach Yourself Setting up a Small Business, Vera Hughes and David Weller (Hodder & Stoughton, 2003)

Teach Yourself Marketing your Small Business, Ros Jay (Hodder & Stoughton, 1996)

Marketing Stripped Bare, Patrick Forsyth (Kogan Page, 2003)

Simply Brilliant, Fergus O'Connell (Prentice Hall, 2001)

Marketing Judo, John Barnes and Richard Richardson (Prentice Hall, 2003)

The End of Marketing as we Know it, Sergio Zyman (HarperCollins, 2000)

Flicking Your Creative Switch, Wayne Lotherington (John Wiley and Sons, 2003)

Achieving Business Alchemy in a Week, Robert Ashton (Hodder & Stoughton, 2002)

Selling In a Week, Christine Harvey (Hodder & Stoughton, 2002)

The Economist Guide to Management Ideas, Tim Hindle (Profile, 2003)

Complete and Unabridged English Dictionary (HarperCollins, 2003)

Self Employment: Making it Work for You, John Spencer and Adrian Pruse (Cassell)

The Evening Standard Big Small Business Guide, Ann Faulkner *et al.* (Gulliver Books, 1996)

The Small Business Action Kit, John Rosthorn *et al.* (Kogan Page, 1994)

index